HOW TO DRAW ANIMATION

HOW TO DRAW ANIMATION

ANIMATION

CHRISTOPHER HART

WATSON-GUPTILL PUBLICATIONS/NEW YORK

For Isabella, Francesca, and, of course, Maria

Senior Editor: Candace Raney
Project Editor: Alisa Palazzo
Designer: Bob Fillie, Graphiti Graphics
Production Manager: Ellen Greene

Front cover art by Christopher Hart
Back cover art by Nancy Beiman

First published in 1997 by Watson-Guptill Publications,
a division of BPI Communications, Inc., 1515 Broadway, New York, N.Y. 10036

Library of Congress Cataloging-in-Publication Data
Hart, Christopher.
    How to draw animation / Christopher Hart.
        p.   cm.
    Includes index.
    ISBN 0-8230-2365-6 (pbk)
1. Animated films—Technique.   I. Title.
NC1765.H326 1997
741.5—dc21   97-13064
                                    CIP

Printed in China

First printing, 1997

3 4 5 6 7 8 9 / 05 04 03 02 01 00 99 98

CONTENTS

ACKNOWLEDGMENTS

Many people have assisted my efforts in bringing this book to fruition. I would like to express my sincere appreciation to them. First, I'd like to express my gratitude to my former classmate, Nancy Beiman, for her helpfulness and generosity of spirit. I'd also like to thank another former classmate and chum, Joe Lansizero, who, incidentally, has the best Hawaiian shirt collection this side of Burbank. A special thanks goes to Roger Allers, co-director of Disney's *The Lion King*, who freely shared his insights in an exclusive interview for this book. I'd also like to thank Christiane Townsend, Trisha Chaves, and the people at MCA Universal Studios; Russell Schroeder at Walt Disney Feature Animation; Cricket Stettinius, Kristen Williams, Richard Betz, and the people at Nickelodeon; Heather Kenyon and the people at Hanna-Barbera, who were so helpful; Linda Simensky, director of programming for The Cartoon Network; and Jim Petropoulos; Bob Fillie, Watson-Guptill's Houdini of book design; Ellen Greene, my production manager; and my editors Candace Raney and Alisa Palazzo, not only for their editorial comments, but for earnestly listening to my suggestions well past the point when anything could be done about them.

CONTRIBUTING ARTISTS

Animation is a broad industry with many specialized positions. No one person does everything. Therefore, in addition to my own work, I've selected some of the finest animation artists in the field to contribute their expertise to this book. Nancy Beiman, supervising animator at Walt Disney Features on the movie *Hercules*; Chrystal Klabunde, lead animator at Warner Brothers Feature Animation on the movie *Quest*; Guy Vasliovich, Creative Director of Development at Film Roman; and Doug Compton, animator on Warner Brothers' Bugs Bunny, Daffy Duck, and Yosemite Sam.

INTRODUCTION

nimation is unparalleled in its ability to capture the hearts and imaginations of audiences, both young and old. It can be zany or poignant. The application of animation is huge in its scope, from movies to television shows, commercials, computer games, and graphics.

This book is abundantly illustrated in an easy-to-follow, step-by-step manner that beginners will appreciate, but it also answers many of the questions that more experienced artists have. It's a comprehensive book that readers can grow with and refer to whenever the need arises. In addition to those people interested in the art of animation, this book is also for those interested in general cartooning, as well as for illustrators who want to improve their understanding of motion, expression, and design. Computer artists, too, who need to know the principles of animation and composition before they can effectively make use of their software programs, will also benefit from the information contained in these pages.

The extensive section on character design includes sections on the dynamics of the face; the art of exaggeration; the evolution of a character; how to create characters based on personality type, and much more. There's also a chapter devoted to period costume design, focusing on styles popularized in animated features.

In the section on anatomy and action analysis, you'll learn how the body reacts to motion, and the different ways that posture is used to define emotions. There is also a thorough section devoted to drawing and animating "realistic" people—the heroes and heroines of animated theatrical feature films. And, you'll also learn about an essential but difficult to locate topic: animal anatomy, with an emphasis on motion and character design.

Animation techniques are covered from beginner through advanced. Most books on this subject only demonstrate how to animate a single character, yet hardly any animated movies feature just one cast member. So accordingly, the secrets of effectively animating *two or more characters* in a scene are revealed. The section on animating dialogue takes the mystery out of this feat and gives you the tools to instill your characters with winning performances.

Layout—the art of staging the scene for maximum impact—is also covered in depth. And as a special feature, included is an exclusive interview with Roger Allers, co-director of Disney's *The Lion King.* In addition to his tremendous insights into the art of animation, he offers suggestions on getting started in the business, what to include in a portfolio, and how to land your first job. You won't want to miss what he has to say.

I hope you enjoy the book, are inspired by it, and, most of all, find it useful. After all, it was written for you.

BASIC PRINCIPLES OF ANIMATION

1 Bear discovers a cache of gold coins.

2 Bear draws back in anticipation *before digging in to scoop up the coins.*

3 The scooping action is bigger and more fun because of the preceding anticipatory motion. Imagine how small the scooping motion would have been had the second step been skipped.

The basic animation principles have been hard won. Early animators worked from scratch to analyze live action in order to imitate it and, ultimately, improve upon it. If you were to create a successive series of drawings *without* utilizing these principles, the result might be animated, but not *convincingly* so. It wouldn't charm or entertain.

Familiarize yourself with these principles as you draw. For me, they hail among the great modern discoveries—right up there with the steam engine and soft taco shells (although you've got to admit, soft taco shells are really in a league of their own).

ANTICIPATION

Anticipation simply means that before a character commits himself by moving in one direction, he first draws back in the opposite direction. It's used for almost all motions in animation—both big and small. The result is a clearer, more emphatic, and "cartoonier" motion.

4 He has hit the jackpot!

Anticipation makes ordinary movements more *dramatic*. Note how the character's whole body gets into the anticipatory movement, even though it's only a short step before the intended motion. It's not meant to take a long beat or to be held. Train your eye to notice anticipation whenever you watch animation.

CHARACTERS MOVE AT DIFFERENT SPEEDS

Tall guys walk more slowly than short guys. Generally, fat characters also move more slowly, and their posture reacts more to their weight than that of thin characters.

If two characters are walking in a scene and covering the same distance in the same time, the smaller character will have to take more steps, and at a faster pace, to keep up with the taller character.

FASTEST WALK
(BABY BEAR)

MEDIUM WALK
(OLDER BROTHER BEAR)

SLOWEST WALK
(PAPA BEAR)

CARICATURING THE ACTION

Most likely, the last time you threw a baseball you didn't jump up in the air with your legs outstretched parallel to the ground. But then again, no one bought a movie ticket to watch you play catch, either. Not so with cartoon characters; they've got an audience that expects to be entertained. One of the joys of animation is the inventiveness of the animators in depicting ordinary actions. Approach each action as a problem to be solved in an entertaining manner, but always in keeping with the character and the story.

LINE OF ACTION

Each figure has its own thrust (or direction), even when it's standing still. This is the character's *line of action.* To strengthen your poses, begin your drawings by using the line of action as a guide. On page119, you'll see how the line of action is essential for animating scenes with two or more characters in them.

SECONDARY ACTION

A secondary action is a movement caused by a previous action, like a chain reaction. In the example of the kangaroo here, the jump is the first action, and the movement of the tail, *which lags a beat behind*, is the secondary action. Other secondary actions in this example involve the ears and the head, which react to the upward and downward forces of the jump.

There's always a delay in secondary actions. Notice that when the kangaroo jumps up, the tail is still in the "down" position. And, when he lands, the tail is still in the "up" position. That's because a secondary action (like that of the tail) happens *second* and is, therefore, a beat behind the original action.

FOLLOW-THROUGH

This is one of the techniques that gives animation its magical quality. Audiences love to watch scenes with lots of follow-through. Follow-through occurs when a secondary action runs its course. In this example, the pooch with the long ears leans forward and stops, but those long ears don't stop with him. They provide a secondary action that *follows through* by swinging back and forth, slowing down like a pendulum, before finally stopping.

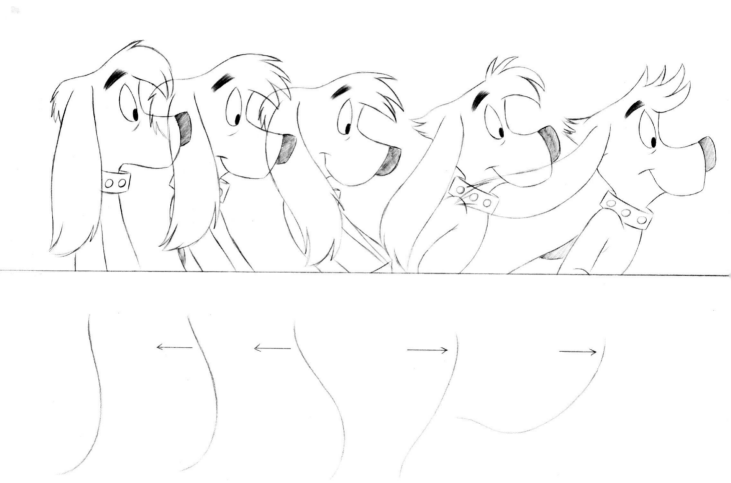

The curved line shows the path of the ear. The arrow shows the direction of the primary action.

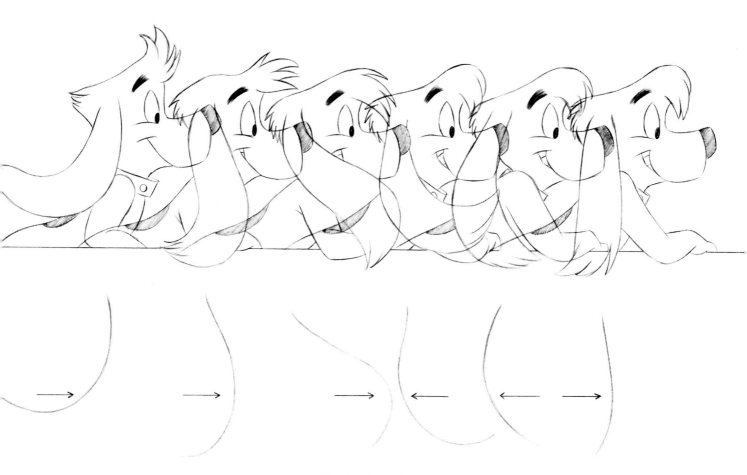

*When the dog stops, the ear
continues to swing back and forth
until it runs out of steam.*

SQUASH AND STRETCH

If you studied live-action films in slow motion, as animators do, you'd notice that the human body actually squashes and stretches when performing different actions. Animated characters squash and stretch all the time—albeit to a much greater degree than actual human bodies. It's as natural to them as breathing is to us.

Heavier characters squash more than thinner ones. By varying the amounts of squash and stretch, you can make one figure seem heavier than another.

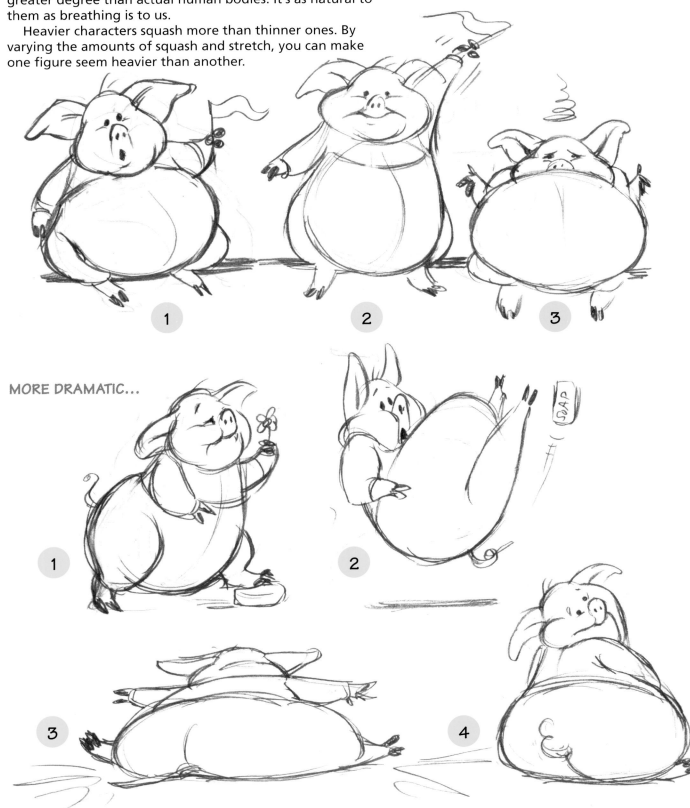

MORE DRAMATIC...

PROPS AND COSTUMES

There's no question that props and costumes help to define a character's personality. While it's possible to draw similar poses for the "generic" character here, the costume identifies the figure as a spy. Note, too, how the clothes help to emphasize the line of action that runs through the body and to show the character's attitude clearly.

Be aware of a character's body under the clothes. You'll achieve more solidity in your drawings if you "draw through" and keep volumes working consistently. Draw through means to draw the parts of the body that are obscured by clothing or other parts of the body, as in the figure at lower left.

A good example of "draw through," note how the figure's right leg is drawn through his left, adding sweep to the pose.

CHARACTER DESIGN

reating appealing characters is the specialty of the character designer, although it's often a collaborative effort by the animators who'll eventually bring those characters to life. I'm sure you've seen movies that have been beautifully animated yet have characters that are ugly or simply uninteresting. In the same way that good acting can't save a bad movie, good animation can't turn an unappealing character into an appealing one. Even villains must have a certain sinister appeal. The best designed characters become the most popular.

HOW TO DRAW EYES

They say that the eyes are the windows to the soul. This is true. However, before you can capture that spark of emotion in the eyes, you must first know a few rules about drawing them. Perspective affects everything in drawing, including the *shape* of the eyes.

FRONT VIEW
In this view, the eyes are the fullest and roundest.

PROFILE
From the side, the eyes are the most slender.

3/4 VIEW
When the head starts to turn, the perspective creates the illusion that the eyes flatten out somewhat. As a result, they take on more of an oval appearance, somewhere between the fullness of a front view and the slenderness of a profile.

You can draw closed eyes in a number of ways:
1. By drawing a single line where the upper and lower lids meet
2. By drawing the upper lid only
3. By drawing both upper and lower lids

CLOSED
Eyes don't have to be open to be highly expressive. Closed eyes can exude a range of emotions, from fury to unbridled joy.

EYEBROWS

Eyebrows are extraordinarily important in creating expressions. They reinforce the emotion behind the eyes. You can achieve a great deal of expression by drawing the eyebrows as if they were a single line. This adds a dynamic flow that is especially appealing in animated characters. By maintaining the single-line approach as an expression changes, you get a nice flow to the transition. Not all eyebrows are drawn as a single line, but it can be an effective tool.

EYES

The shape and shine of the eyes, and even the pupils themselves, can change drastically according to the facial expression. Below are some examples of popular techniques.

Eyeballs can lead when looking.

Light source puts a shine (or highlight) at upper right.

Even when eyeballs change position, the shine stays in the same place due to the light source.

Eyeballs enlarge in expressions of innocence. Eyes can also suddenly sprout lashes.

Eyeballs shrink in fearful expressions.

Eyes merge into one shape to show extreme, comical fear or surprise.

Many emotions, such as fatigue, can only be conveyed by partially covering the eyes with upper eyelids.

Increase the size of a shine for stunned, blank-stare expressions.

Symbols can be used in place of the eyeballs to reveal inner thoughts.

EYELIDS
Eyelids can also help create an expression or convey emotion.

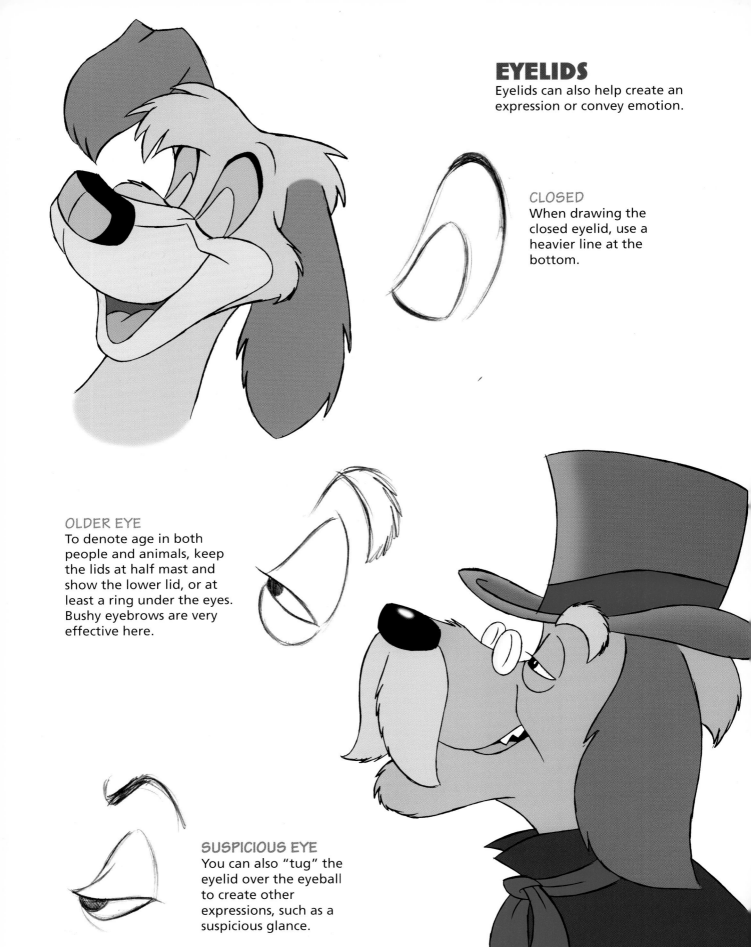

CLOSED
When drawing the closed eyelid, use a heavier line at the bottom.

OLDER EYE
To denote age in both people and animals, keep the lids at half mast and show the lower lid, or at least a ring under the eyes. Bushy eyebrows are very effective here.

SUSPICIOUS EYE
You can also "tug" the eyelid over the eyeball to create other expressions, such as a suspicious glance.

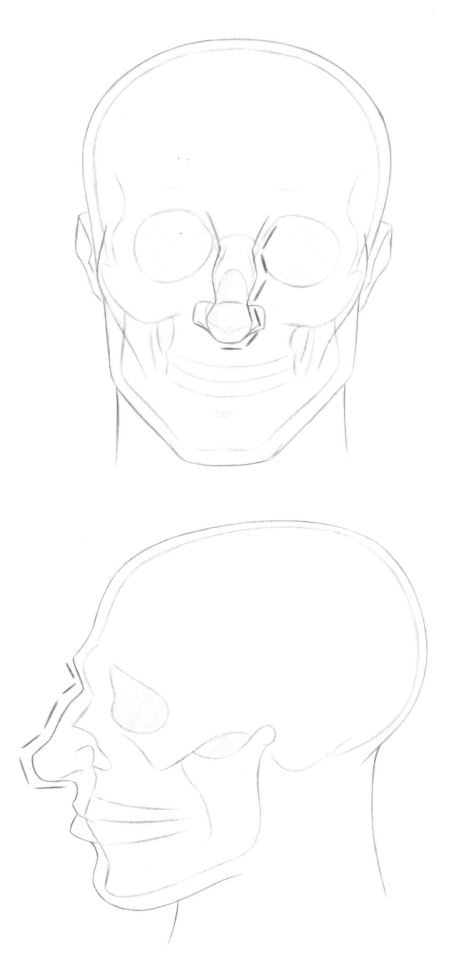

HOW TO DRAW THE NOSE

People don't generally think of the nose as an expressive element of the face, but it's a very distinctive feature because of its unparalleled prominence. The bridge of the nose is made up of bone, with the rest of the nose being cartilage. There's a narrowing in the middle of the nose where the bone meets the cartilage, and a separate group of cartilage makes up the tip of the nose, which is why it gets larger at the end.

Note all the angles in the profile. (This will become second nature to you quickly.) It's important to study the angles of the nose, indicated here in red. Cartoony noses can be flat or round, and in these cases, the angles are pretty much nonexistent. However, when you begin to draw characters with some realism, such as the heroes and heroines of animated feature films, you'll need to understand the construction.

Take a look in the mirror at your own nose. Pretty scary, huh? If you touch the bridge of your nose, you'll be able to feel where the cartilage begins because it's malleable. You'll also notice many of the angles that are shown in the diagram, although they may be more subtle on you. Real life is always a great reference tool. Animators often keep mirrors on their desks for guidance in creating expressions.

THE BRIDGE OF THE NOSE

There's a shift in angle where the bone (bridge of the nose) meets the cartilage. How high up on the head you place that break is a creative decision that influences the look of a character. In extreme cases, you could even place the break above the eyes.

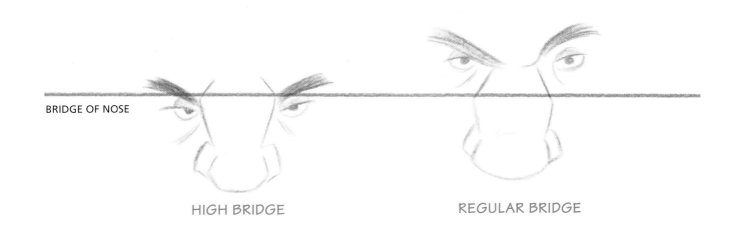

BRIDGE OF NOSE

HIGH BRIDGE

REGULAR BRIDGE

THE NOSE IN PROFILE

By merely changing the shape of the nose, you can change the look of a character. Knowing how to construct an average nose will increase your ability to invent different types. Not every angle of the nose will be clearly defined in all cases; you can eliminate some angles and exaggerate others to create a more unique look.

THE JAW

The jaw is the unsung hero of character design. By making clever use of this feature, you can invent many creative and winning characters.

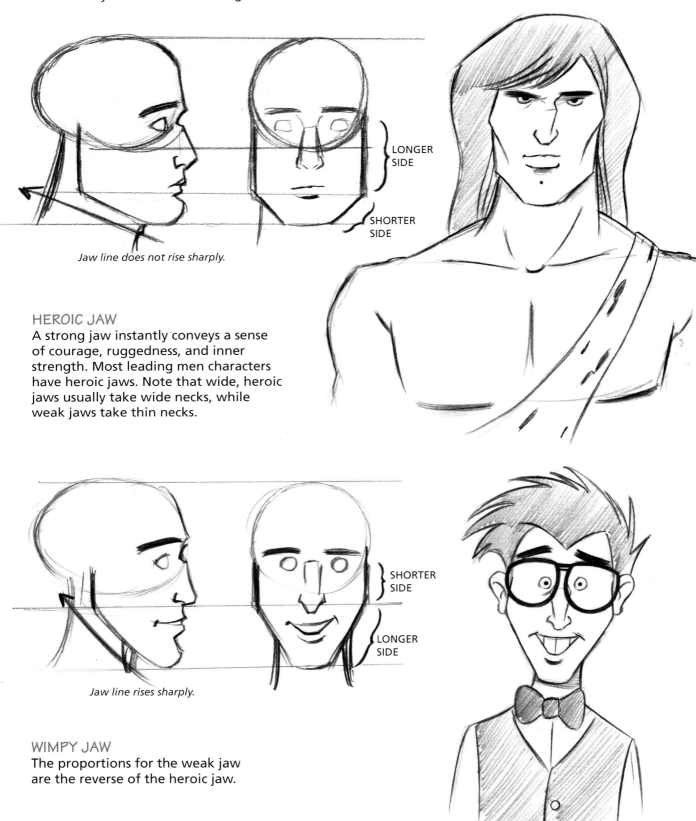

LONGER SIDE

SHORTER SIDE

Jaw line does not rise sharply.

HEROIC JAW

A strong jaw instantly conveys a sense of courage, ruggedness, and inner strength. Most leading men characters have heroic jaws. Note that wide, heroic jaws usually take wide necks, while weak jaws take thin necks.

SHORTER SIDE

LONGER SIDE

Jaw line rises sharply.

WIMPY JAW

The proportions for the weak jaw are the reverse of the heroic jaw.

THE PRONOUNCED JAW

Pronounced jaws make for some of the funniest characters on the screen. Just like people, jaws come in all shapes and sizes.

This wacky old guy has a typical, exaggerated cartoon jaw. The chin curves around and back into the mouth. Where the jowl meets the chin, there is an indentation.

A woman can have a pronounced jaw and still look attractive. It creates a self-satisfied, rich look. The jaw here is rounded, without sharp angles.

Most burly characters have a chin that juts outward while the jaw swings forward in a strong curve.

THE WEAK JAW

As expressive as strong jaws are, weak jaws can help to create wonderfully eccentric personalities, too.

The typical weak jaw recedes from the point of the lower lip.

Sometimes, the jaw is eliminated altogether, and the lower lip melds into the line of the neck.

Sometimes a weak jaw is buried in a fat neck.

Animal jaws are often drawn with the lower part of the chin wider than the top. This is especially true with big cats.

Some animals are typecast and, therefore, will always be drawn with big jaws, such as the bully of the dog world—the bulldog.

Because of their particular anatomy, some animals can have huge jaws without appearing rugged at all, as in the pelican.

THE DYNAMICS OF THE FACE

SQUASH AND STRETCH

Just as you use the principle of *squash and stretch* for animating the body, you also use it to create expressions for the face. Designing an animated character means more than simply drawing an appealing face; it means drawing a face that can move, constrict, and stretch.

The face will literally squash down or stretch up, depending on the expression. Frowns and smiles generally compress the face, while surprise and fear generally elongate it. Also, rounder, cartoonier characters will exhibit more squash and stretch than realistically drawn ones.

Note that the face doesn't remain in the squashed or stretched position indefinitely. It stays there for only a moment, and then resumes its normal shape.

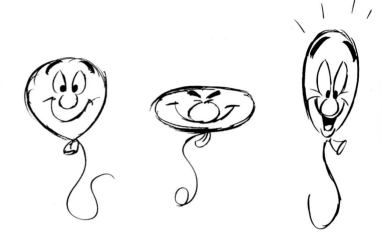

CRUSH AND STRETCH

A more sophisticated and specific type of squash and stretch is *crush and stretch.* In a smile or frown, as one side of the face crushes down with the eyebrow, the same side of the mouth rises up to meet it. Conversely, the other eyebrow rises, and the mouth on that side lowers as a counterbalance. This is very important in feature-style animation, in which these expressions are used frequently.

Face crushes on left side, stretches on right.

Face crushes on right side, stretches on left.

TUGGING

To squeeze out an extra expression, "tug" the mouth to one side of the face, as demonstrated on this annoyed king character. Note that the face is still crushing on one side and stretching on the other.

FACIAL WRINKLES

Wrinkles in the face are caused by the regular flexing of facial muscles. When people make expressions, they're flexing their facial muscles. Think of expressions as muscles thrusting in a direction, and think of the wrinkles as the reaction to those forces.

When the mouth widens into a smile, it pushes the crease lines around the cheeks out, the same way this finger stretches this line. The points where the force of the mouth meets the cheek will show the most reaction.

The face has many muscles. A down-turned mouth is caused by the muscles below the lower lip and in the chin.

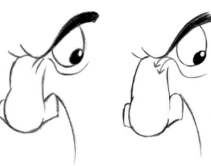

SNARL WRINKLES

The snarl wrinkle travels from under the eye to the bridge of the nose and is crushed by the eyebrow.

LINE FLOW

Instead of accurately portraying the crease lines from the nose to the mouth, and then drawing a separate set of crease lines from the lips to the chin, it's more pleasing to simplify everything. Just join the creases to form one long line from the nose down to the chin.

Accurate version.   *Simplified version.*

THE SNARL

The snarl is a great facial expression. It's most typically thought of as representing anger or annoyance, but it's useful as an accent to other, more benign expressions, as well. Think of it as adding a bit of spice. The typical snarl illustrated here gives the smile its edge.

On humans, and especially on animals, snarl wrinkles start at the crease around the mouth and loop up around the bridge of the nose, where several forces converge into an expressive pattern of wrinkles.

SECONDARY WRINKLES

Some wrinkles are caused by other wrinkles; these are *secondary wrinkles.* Be careful not to overdo the wrinkles. This bear below has three secondary wrinkles: two over his mouth creases and one over his eyebrow. Any more than that would start to make this fellow ugly. If you need a lot of wrinkles to convey an expression, you should probably revise it so that it's more effective with fewer lines.

CONTRACTION

The face contracts or expands depending on its expression. This horse's grimace contracts the face —everything converges toward a single point.

THE SMILE

There's no such thing as a simple smile. An innocent smile on one person can mean something sinister on another. There are happy smiles, melancholy smiles, nervous and embarrassed smiles—in fact, there are as many smiles as there are moods.

Expressions are tools that animators use to articulate moods, some of which can be quite complex. Before you draw an expression, be it a smile, frown, or anything else, try to capture the subtleties of the mood in the expression. Placing a generic smile on a character's face does a disservice to the writer's intentions. Consider what's going on underneath that smile. What are you, the animator, trying to convey with a smile? For example, is the smile genuine or forced?

To see some of the best examples of expressions, take a good look at Jackie Gleason in the original black-and-white television show, *The Honeymooners.* It's especially useful to watch the show with the sound off so that you're focusing only on the physical performance. His use of timing, exaggeration, intention, and subtext is nothing less than masterful. Although a large man, he was one of the truly gifted physical comedians; his entire body lurched with every pose and gesture. He could hold an expression for just the right amount of time to break up an audience. A smile from him could mean overconfidence, boyish innocence, or vengeful glee.

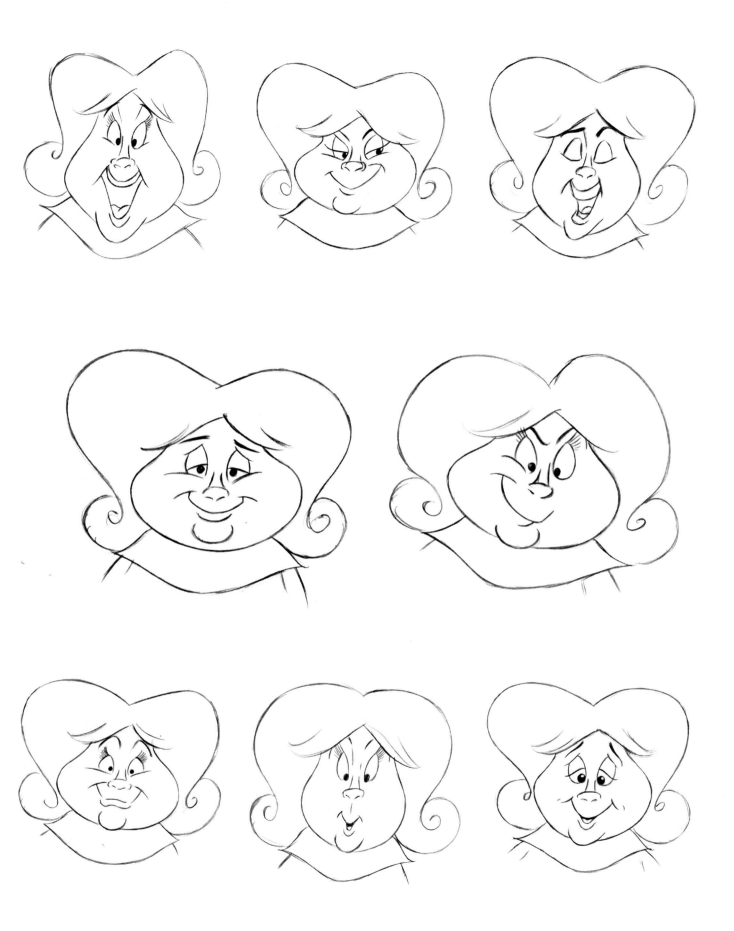

PUSHING AN EXPRESSION

Don't settle for the ordinary. By "tweaking," or *pushing,* a character's facial expression, you get that extra energy and vitality that can make a moment memorable.

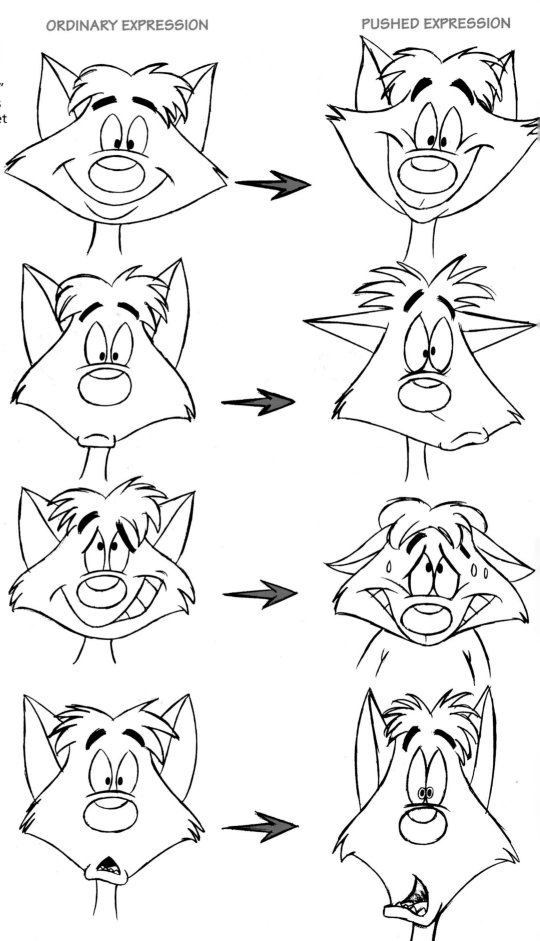

REVERSE CURVES

Have you noticed that professional animators impart a special quality to their drawings that most other cartoonists lack? That special flair is called a *reverse curve*. This is important! It adds a graceful flow to the line, which is one of the most appealing aspects of a winning cartoon character. Here's how to make use of it in your drawings.

The reverse curve is a line that curves, but instead of continuing in the path of the curve, it curves back again in the opposite direction.

The reverse curves on this lady's head have all been highlighted. Each one adds a graceful flow to the drawing, which would otherwise be stiff.

CHARMING AND YOUNG CHARACTERS

I know, I know . . . this section is supposed to explain facial dynamics. But while we're on the subject of reverse curves, it's important to expand into using this technique on the body, as well.

Reverse curves are essential in creating a sympathetic line for the tummy on charming and youthful characters. Compare the two bears here. Notice how stiff the bear on the left, without the reverse curves, is. The reverse curves give the bear on the right weight and momentum—two important features for any animated character.

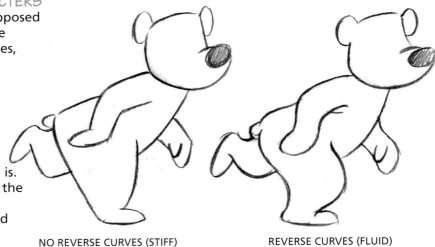

NO REVERSE CURVES (STIFF)   REVERSE CURVES (FLUID)

Notice reverse curve from chest to legs.

CHARACTERS BUILT ON A SINGLE FEATURE

There are many ways to create a new character. Some artists choose a well-known celebrity as a starting point. Because a performer's personality is evident from his or her performances, artists have an attitude from which to work. They then continue to make small changes in the drawing until the character becomes an original creation. At other times, free association drawing will produce an inspired sketch that can be honed and crafted.

Another effective method of development is to build a character on the basis of one primary feature, which should be caricatured, as illustrated here. This gives the character a focal point. If you greatly exaggerate more than one primary feature, you run the risk of having too many elements competing against one another.

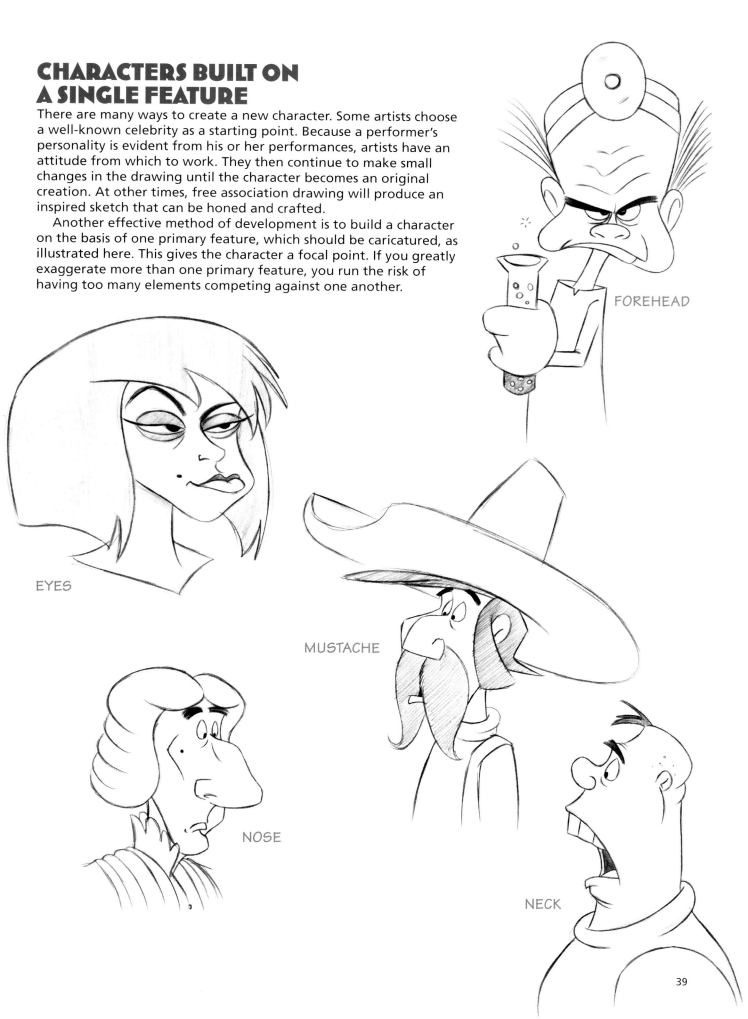

FOREHEAD

EYES

MUSTACHE

NOSE

NECK

ANATOMY AND ACTION ANALYSIS

In order to draw and animate human figures for feature films, you must have a working knowledge of anatomy. It was discovered long ago that the rubbery, big-nose type of animated cartoon characters that sustained the audience's interest in short films would not hold the audience's attention for an hour and a half. More realism was required.

Practice in life drawing is recommended, but unlike painters, animation artists cannot do all of their drawing from models. They must be able to draw from their imagination. Therefore, they've devised methods to arrive at anatomically correct figures. Even though the human skeleton is a very complicated structure, you can greatly simplify it when blocking out, or analyzing motion.

The most important things to keep in mind are what bends and where. Notice the hinging of elbows, wrists, knees, and ankles. Learn to recognize the special motion of the ball-and-socket joints of the shoulders and hips. Make use of the flexibility of the spine (but remember that the spine doesn't stretch and compress—it simply increases or decreases in amount of curve).

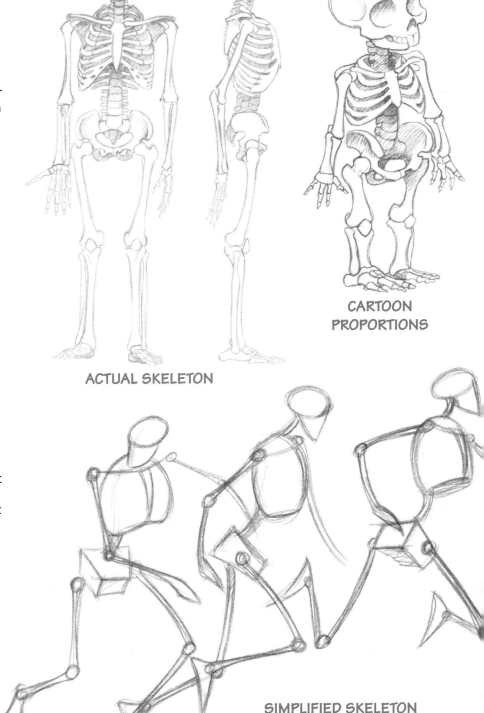

CARTOON PROPORTIONS

ACTUAL SKELETON

SIMPLIFIED SKELETON FOR ANIMATION

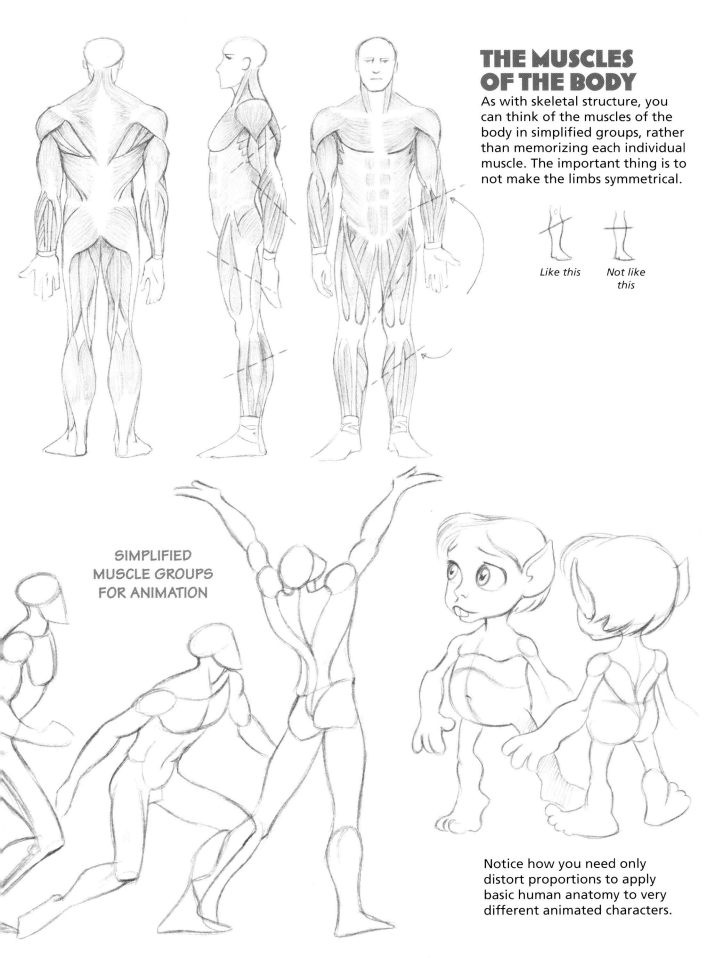

THE MUSCLES OF THE BODY

As with skeletal structure, you can think of the muscles of the body in simplified groups, rather than memorizing each individual muscle. The important thing is to not make the limbs symmetrical.

Like this   *Not like this*

SIMPLIFIED MUSCLE GROUPS FOR ANIMATION

Notice how you need only distort proportions to apply basic human anatomy to very different animated characters.

DRAWING THE HEAD FROM DIFFERENT ANGLES

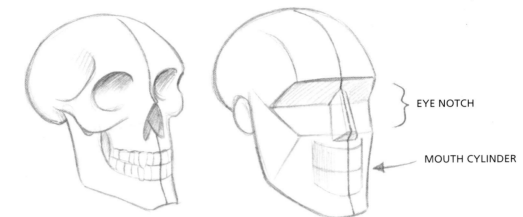

EYE NOTCH

MOUTH CYLINDER

BASIC HEAD CONSTRUCTION

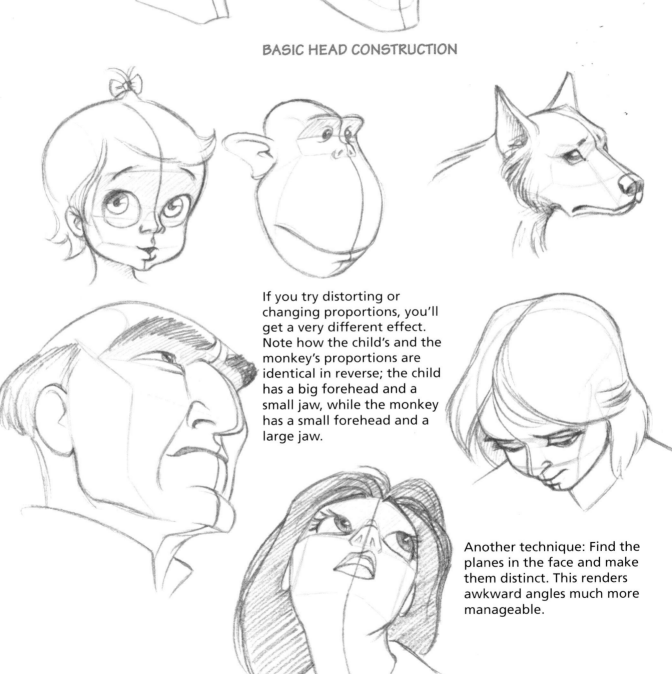

If you try distorting or changing proportions, you'll get a very different effect. Note how the child's and the monkey's proportions are identical in reverse; the child has a big forehead and a small jaw, while the monkey has a small forehead and a large jaw.

Another technique: Find the planes in the face and make them distinct. This renders awkward angles much more manageable.

HAND CONSTRUCTION

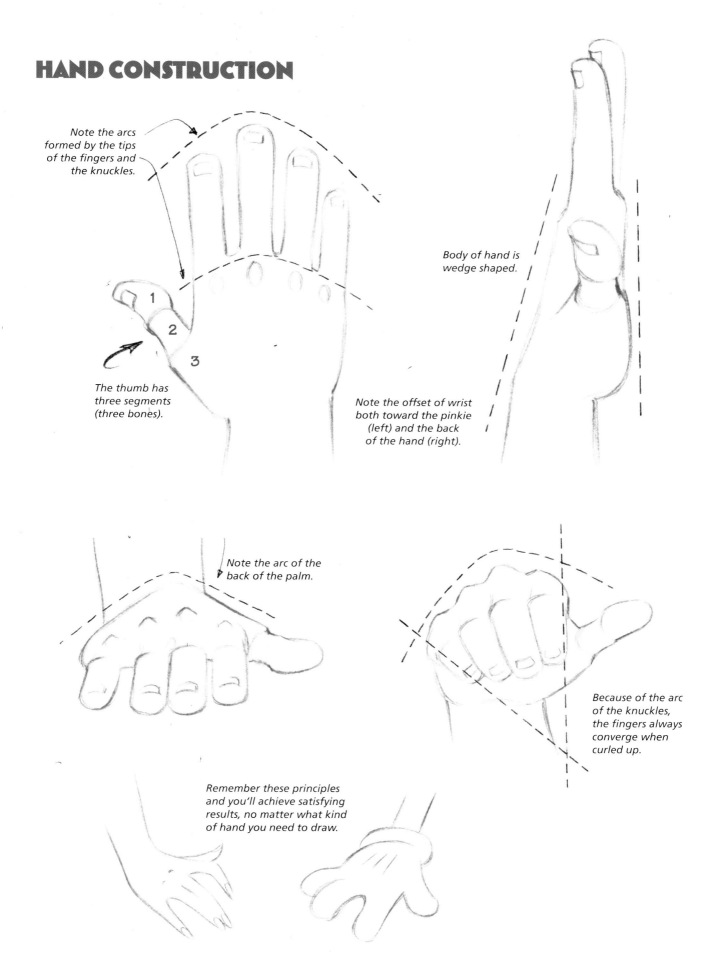

Note the arcs formed by the tips of the fingers and the knuckles.

The thumb has three segments (three bones).

Body of hand is wedge shaped.

Note the offset of wrist both toward the pinkie (left) and the back of the hand (right).

Note the arc of the back of the palm.

Because of the arc of the knuckles, the fingers always converge when curled up.

Remember these principles and you'll achieve satisfying results, no matter what kind of hand you need to draw.

FOOT CONSTRUCTION

There are two kinds of people: those who can draw feet, and those who can't. Within these two groups lie all known subsets: tall, short, red headed, skinny, and so on.

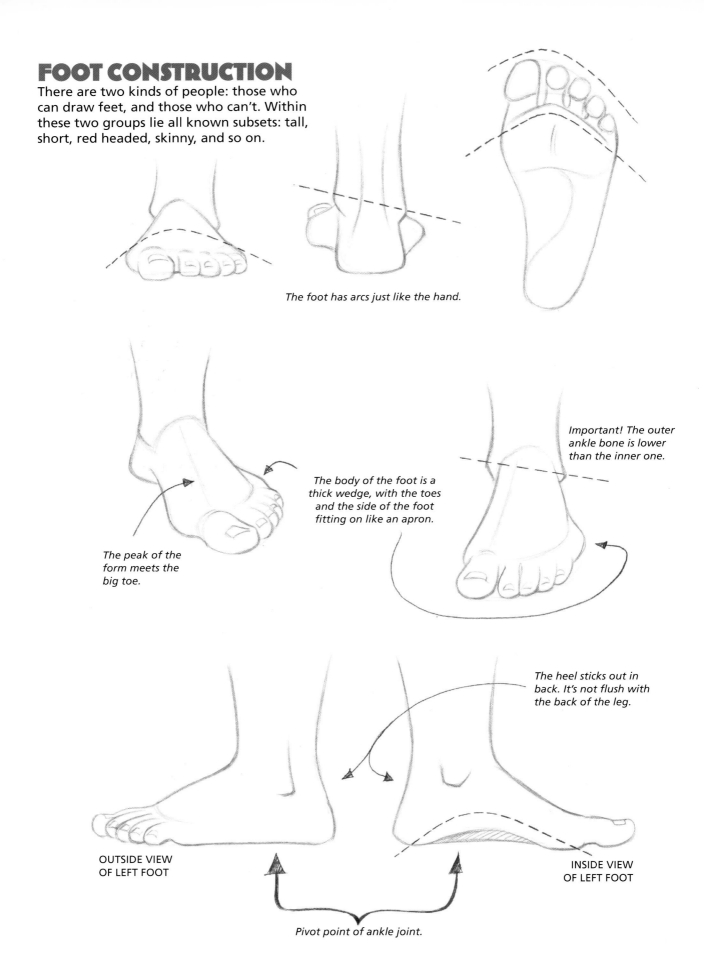

The foot has arcs just like the hand.

The peak of the form meets the big toe.

The body of the foot is a thick wedge, with the toes and the side of the foot fitting on like an apron.

Important! The outer ankle bone is lower than the inner one.

The heel sticks out in back. It's not flush with the back of the leg.

OUTSIDE VIEW
OF LEFT FOOT

INSIDE VIEW
OF LEFT FOOT

Pivot point of ankle joint.

USING OVERLAPPING LINES TO CREATE DIMENSION

Everyone wants three things in life:

1. To be rich

2. To drive a great foreign sports car

3. To create animated characters that have a feeling of roundness

I may not be able to help you with the first two, but for the third one, you've come to the right place. By drawing one line overlapping another, you create the illusion of distance. You can see this when looking at rolling hills in a landscape. When drawing figures, think of the muscles as those rolling hills—one group of muscles overlapping another. By drawing the overlap, you create a more three-dimensional shape. Without this, a drawing will appear flat. Note how the elbow of the figure here appears to come forward, while the shoulder seems to recede. It's all due to the overlapping lines.

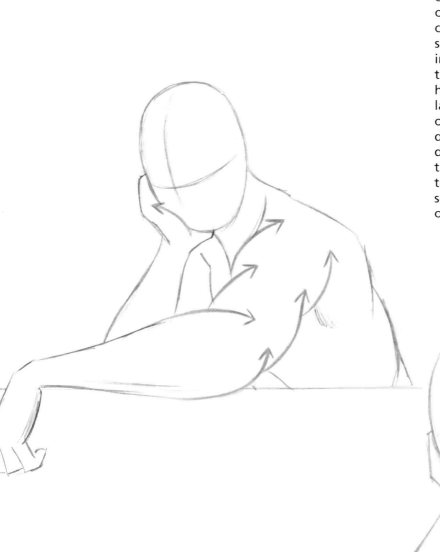

Objects that are nearer the viewer always overlap objects that are further away. This sounds simple in principle, but the human body, as well as the animal body, has many subtle twists and turns. It takes a conscious study of the figure to accurately "see" which lines are in front and which are further back.

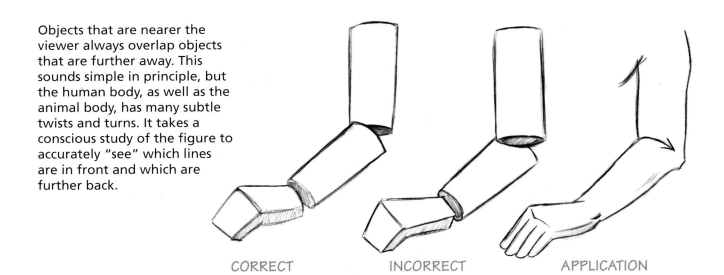

CORRECT   INCORRECT   APPLICATION

Overlapping is a principle used for drawing all types of figures, including very round, cartoony characters. As with all figures, the effectiveness of the characters here would be lost without the overlapping lines.

THE SIDES OF THE FIGURE

Another way to avoid creating a character that appears flat is to make sure that your figure has *sides.* The arms on this figure aren't attached to the front of his body, but to his *sides.* So, you need to draw the torso not as a flat rectangle, but as a box with dimension. The arms go on the narrow side panels of the box.

Of course, the rectangular box is only a guideline and doesn't appear in the final drawing. However, you can still give your viewer a sense of this box. For example, look at the slope of this figure's shoulders; it represents the top of the box, which recedes toward the background.

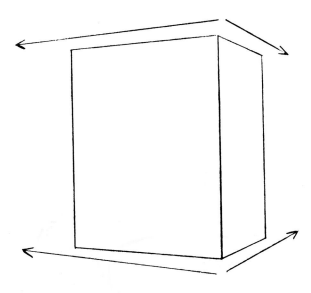

DRAW WITH FEELING

Even though the character works nicely as a whole unit, if you look at the preceding page, you will see that it is actually a compilation of different pieces. The question then becomes: How do you create a drawing out of pieces and not have it look like a lifeless jigsaw puzzle? The answer is that you must keep in mind the overall *feeling* of the character, especially its personality. Keep referring to that spark of inspiration, while checking your anatomy along the way. You are drawing a feeling, not a sterile image. You want your character to accurately convey that feeling to others through its personality, be it charm, wickedness, or anything else.

Before I put pencil to paper, I start with the feeling, but at some point, the drawing takes over and becomes almost a sentient being. It seems to direct the show. It "wants" to be cuter or sneakier or funnier. I try to help it become more of what it wants to be. When I'm finished, I'll look at the drawing, and if it doesn't instantly give me that feeling, I'll redraw it until it does.

The worst character is a lifeless one. Anatomy is only a tool; Feeling and imagination are the keys. Trust your gut and draw with feeling.

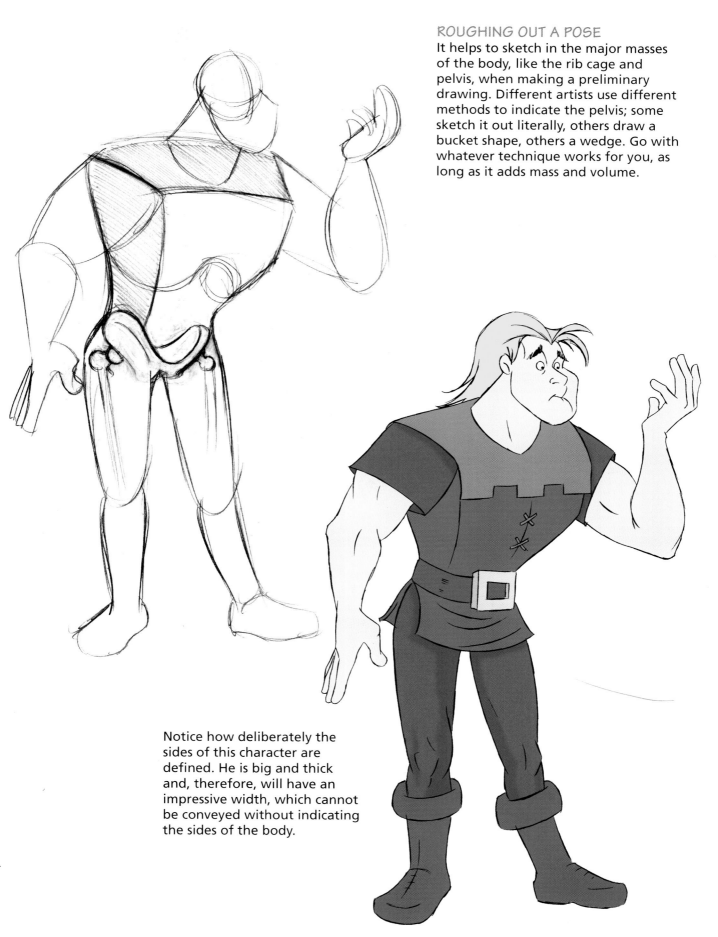

ROUGHING OUT A POSE
It helps to sketch in the major masses of the body, like the rib cage and pelvis, when making a preliminary drawing. Different artists use different methods to indicate the pelvis; some sketch it out literally, others draw a bucket shape, others a wedge. Go with whatever technique works for you, as long as it adds mass and volume.

Notice how deliberately the sides of this character are defined. He is big and thick and, therefore, will have an impressive width, which cannot be conveyed without indicating the sides of the body.

DYNAMIC POSES— TWISTING THE TORSO

Animators are always trying to wring a bit more feeling out of a pose. One way to do this is to twist the torso and hips (rib cage and pelvis) in opposite directions. This adds a dynamic element to what might otherwise be a static pose.

By twisting the torso of the figure here, two things happen: one arm and shoulder come forward, and one arm and shoulder move back. This is more interesting than having the figure face the viewer squarely. The pose now has a feeling of energy in it.

Note how the center line continues down the middle of the chest and pelvis, even as the figure twists.

Twisting the torso and hips in opposite directions adds a bit of gracefulness to heroic poses.

These two ladies are gossiping about someone and, man, is it juicy! Twisting the torso and hips keeps the figures from looking stiff, like statues. In comic strips, stiff poses are okay because the images are reduced to such small sizes in the newspaper, where simpler poses read better. (In addition, lack of motion in a comic strip is interpreted as droll restraint.) But for movie and television audiences, stiff animation, unless highly stylized or hilariously written, comes across as a cheap effort.

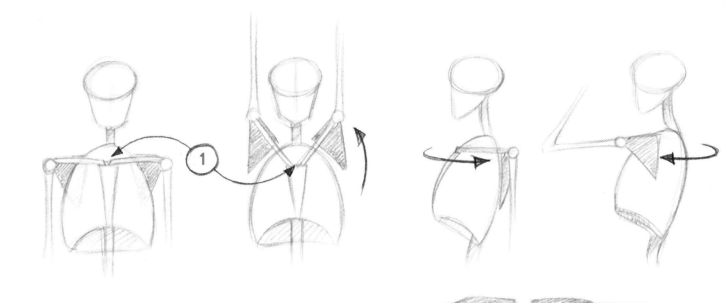

SHOULDER MOTION

The motion of the shoulder is often misunderstood. The chest is *not* a square box with the arms sticking right out of the corners, no matter which way the figure is reaching. Amazingly, the only point where the shoulder bones actually connect to the main skeleton is at the spot where the clavicle, or collar bone, meets the sternum, or breast bone (see number 1 above). The scapula (shoulder blade) moves around freely and can assume some surprising positions.

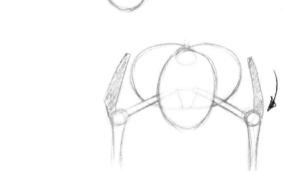

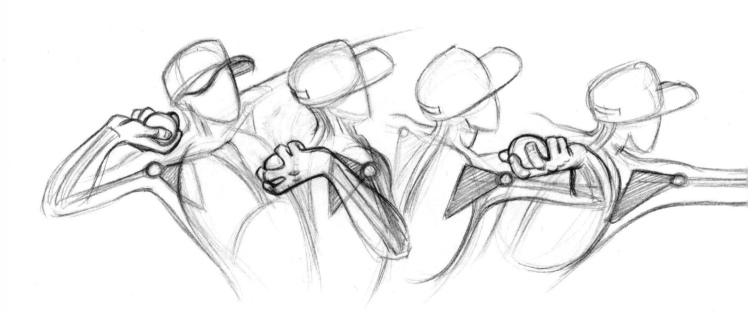

BODY LANGUAGE

Notice how, in a "natural" stance, the spine arches comfortably, the plane of the top of the chest angles so that the neck sticks slightly forward, and the pelvis tilts down somewhat. Compare this to the "unnatural" stance, seen so often in Saturday-morning cartoon animation.

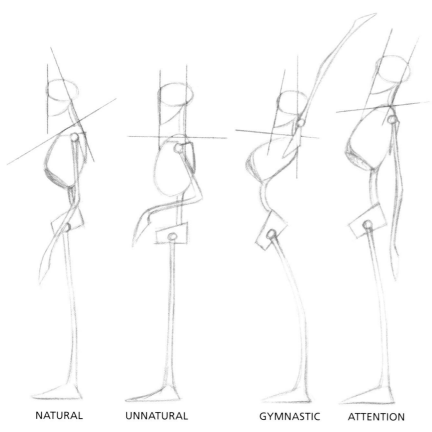

NATURAL   UNNATURAL   GYMNASTIC   ATTENTION   SAD   AGED

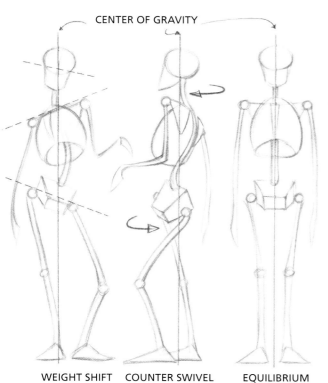

CENTER OF GRAVITY

WEIGHT SHIFT   COUNTER SWIVEL   EQUILIBRIUM

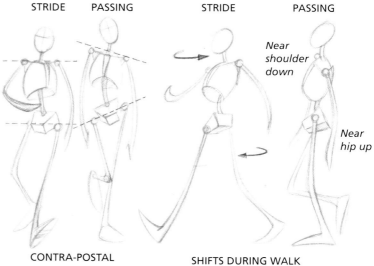

STRIDE   PASSING   STRIDE   PASSING

Near shoulder down

Near hip up

CONTRA-POSTAL   SHIFTS DURING WALK

HOW THE BODY SHIFTS DURING THE WALK

Here are some examples of how the body compensates for shifts of weight and balance. The lines mark the plane of the top of the chest, and the plane of the pelvis. Note that the position of the pelvis, the arch of the spine, and whether the knees are bent or locked straight all change at different stages of the walking motion.

ANIMATING THE HUMAN WALK

Animators don't often draw an action from beginning to end, all in order. Since drawing is an imperfect science, the first drawing of the character would look quite different from the hundredth. Unconsciously, the animator would subtly start to change the character, perhaps making it shorter or fatter or with slightly bigger feet.

To solve this problem, animators draw the most important poses within the action first, which are called the *extremes.* Then, they draw the *breakdown* poses, which are the stances that occur between the extremes. And finally, they fill in the drawings that go between (and connect) the extremes and the breakdowns; these are the *in-betweens.*

When animating a walk, start with the stride positions (poses 17 and 33 below), and draw as many strides as you need, lining them up footprint to footprint. Next, draw the passing positions (poses 9 and 21), placing them right between your stride extremes. Then add the breakdown stances (poses 5, 13, 21, and 29).

Now all that's left are the in-betweens. Pay special attention to foot action; for example, when you create, say, pose 15, the left heel may still be

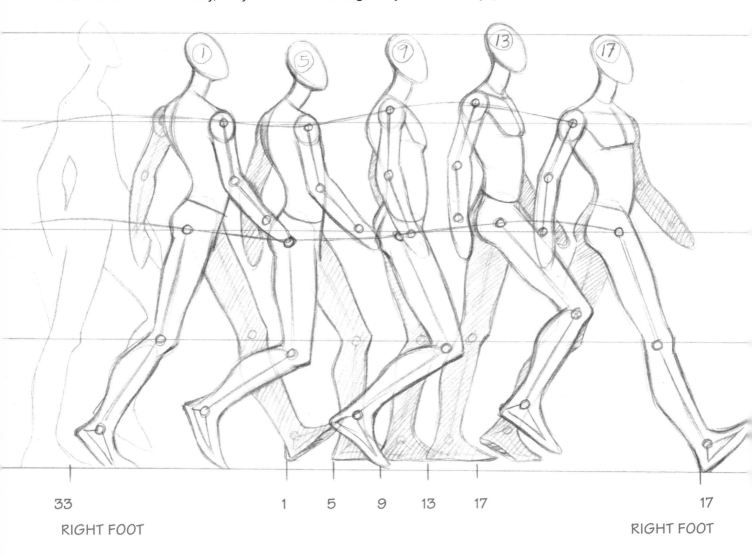

33

RIGHT FOOT

1 5 9 13 17

17

RIGHT FOOT

down on the ground and the right knee may be quite high. Try lots of different things; this illustration shows only one type of walk. For example, try keeping the feet on the ground longer, as if the character was very heavy, or try changing the timing in other ways. The walk cycle illustrated here takes 32 drawings, and it begins to repeat itself at drawing 33. You can put in more or fewer in-betweens as you see fit, or you could give the figure a limp by making the timing uneven.

Note the wave motion in the walk, which is the result of a few things:

1. The up and down movement of the body.
2. The tilts of the shoulders and hips. The weight-bearing hip is higher than the other, and the shoulder on the same side is also raised for balance. Note, too, how the waistline tips from side to side.
3. The rotations of the shoulders and hips. The red dots in the shoulder bunch up and spread out over the course of the walk; they bunch in figures 1 to 17, then spread from figures 17 to 33.
4. The swing of arms and legs. Bunching and spreading is even more obvious here.

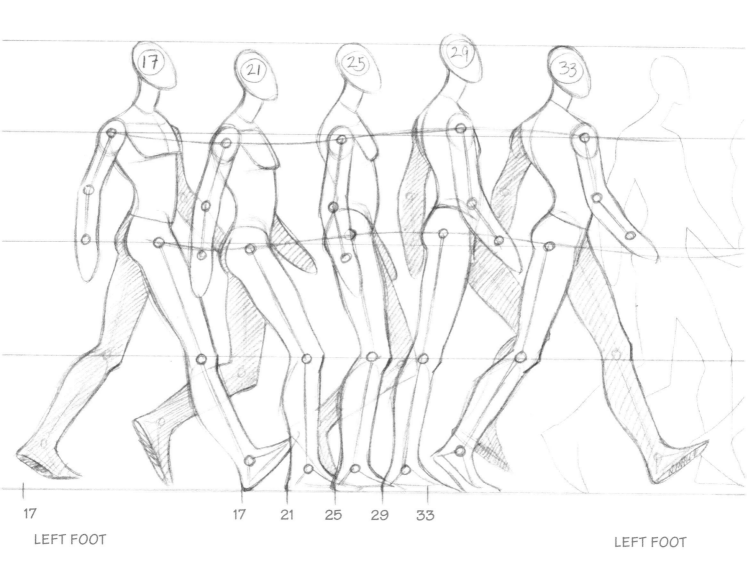

17

LEFT FOOT

17   21   25   29   33

LEFT FOOT

THE FAT WALK

Many of the same principles of a simple human walk apply to cartoonier versions. However, you can and should modify your walks according to your character's body type and personality.

For example, this fat character is so big that he sways from side to side as he walks. He also exhibits a great deal of *squash and stretch* as he rises and lands.

THE FAST RUN

A fast run doesn't always necessitate a forward-leaning body, but a backward-leaning body in a fast run will tend toward silliness, which may or may not be the effect you have in mind. Also with this type of run, don't let the up-and-down motion of the character become too extreme, or it will cancel out the forward movement. Notice, too, that the legs hit their full extension a beat before the arms hit theirs. In this example, one stride covers four drawings, 8 and 1, and 4 and 5. And, drawings 2 and 3, and 6 and 7 represent the "step through."

Another thing to note: The drag on drawings 3 and 7—the foot that's rapidly stepping through the motion drags back in the path of action, creating a semi-blur.

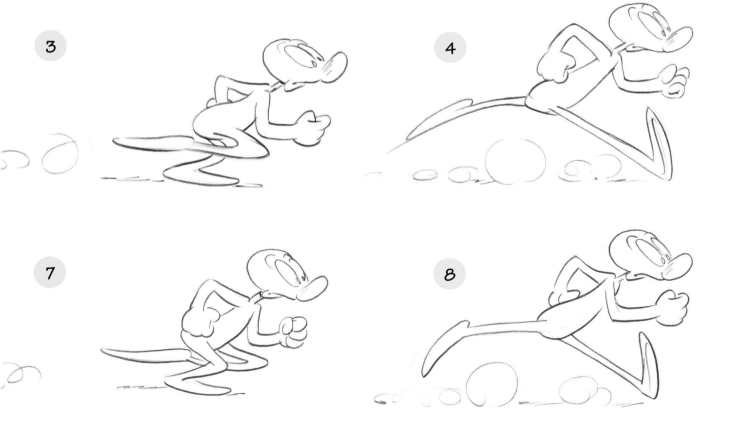

ANIMAL ANATOMY, GAITS, AND DESIGN

It's important to keep a reference file on hand for drawing animals. If you don't, you'll just be drawing cartoon animals based on your recollections of other cartoon animals, and your drawings will show a lack of mastery. The next time you go to a zoo, bring along a sketchbook, and add any sketches you make to your reference file.

You'll get the best understanding of animal anatomy by comparing the joints of animals to similar joints in humans.

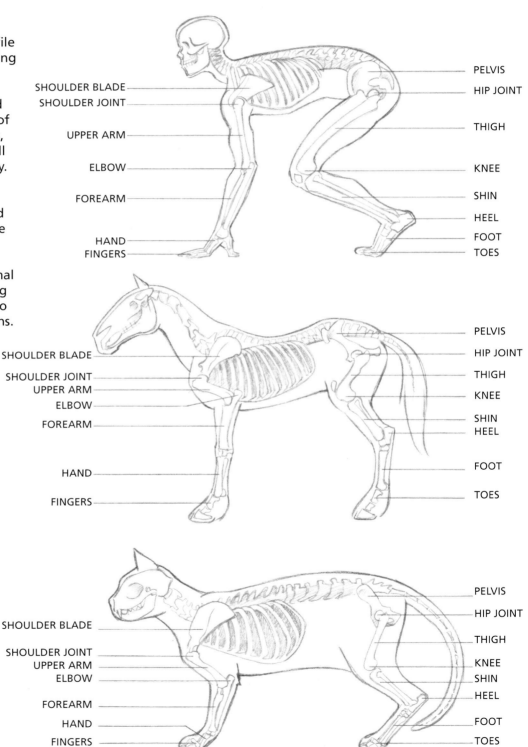

SHOULDER BLADE
SHOULDER JOINT
UPPER ARM
ELBOW
FOREARM
HAND
FINGERS

PELVIS
HIP JOINT
THIGH
KNEE
SHIN
HEEL
FOOT
TOES

SHOULDER BLADE
SHOULDER JOINT
UPPER ARM
ELBOW
FOREARM
HAND
FINGERS

PELVIS
HIP JOINT
THIGH
KNEE
SHIN
HEEL
FOOT
TOES

SHOULDER BLADE
SHOULDER JOINT
UPPER ARM
ELBOW
FOREARM
HAND
FINGERS

PELVIS
HIP JOINT
THIGH
KNEE
SHIN
HEEL
FOOT
TOES

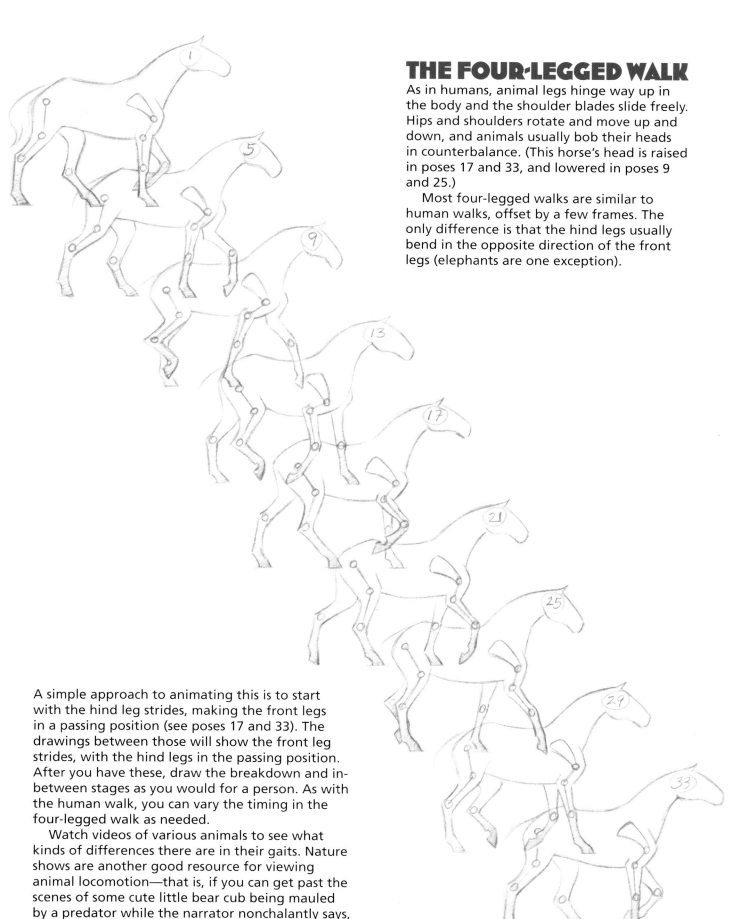

THE FOUR-LEGGED WALK

As in humans, animal legs hinge way up in the body and the shoulder blades slide freely. Hips and shoulders rotate and move up and down, and animals usually bob their heads in counterbalance. (This horse's head is raised in poses 17 and 33, and lowered in poses 9 and 25.)

Most four-legged walks are similar to human walks, offset by a few frames. The only difference is that the hind legs usually bend in the opposite direction of the front legs (elephants are one exception).

A simple approach to animating this is to start with the hind leg strides, making the front legs in a passing position (see poses 17 and 33). The drawings between those will show the front leg strides, with the hind legs in the passing position. After you have these, draw the breakdown and in-between stages as you would for a person. As with the human walk, you can vary the timing in the four-legged walk as needed.

Watch videos of various animals to see what kinds of differences there are in their gaits. Nature shows are another good resource for viewing animal locomotion—that is, if you can get past the scenes of some cute little bear cub being mauled by a predator while the narrator nonchalantly says, "It may seem cruel, but it's nature's way."

THE ANIMAL WALK—UP CLOSE

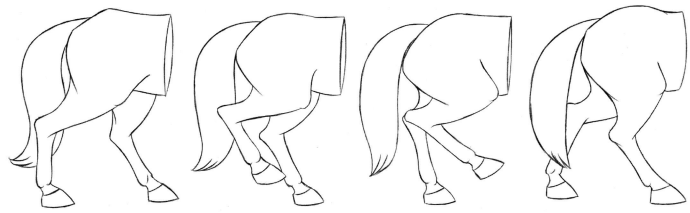

WRONG (above)

The legs are stiff. The joints don't seem to bend. The horse's right hoof looks like it has been soldered onto the leg. Remember the principles of flow and drag.

RIGHT (below)

Notice how the right hoof now drags behind when the horse lifts it off the ground. Note, too, how the body shifts slightly, swaying toward us when the right leg is back and away from us when the right leg moves forward. These same shifts occur in the body with the foreleg motion.

FOOT LEVELS

When animating four-legged animals, it's important to maintain two different foot levels. This horse's right side is slightly farther from us than his left side, which is closer. Because of perspective, the closer legs will appear slightly longer and the more distant legs, slightly shorter. If you were to draw this horse with all of its hooves on the same plane, it would look as though it were walking on a tight rope.

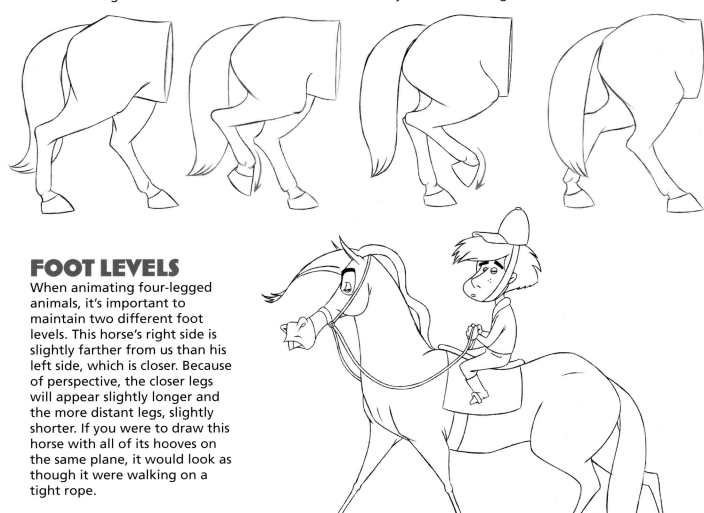

FAR SIDE

NEAR SIDE

THE FOUR-LEGGED RUN

The cat provides an good example of a very flexible four-legged run. Notice the following in the various stages of the run illustrated here:

1. How the back arches, even reversing its arc (poses 1 and 13).

2. The extreme range of the hind legs, from almost straight forward (pose 7) to almost straight back (pose 13).

3. How far the shoulder blade slides, reaching way ahead of the chest (pose 1), then pushing above the back when it absorbs the body's weight (pose 4).

4. The spring action of the hind legs as they propel the body (pose 10).

The smaller an animal is, the faster is will move. This cat is running on 15s (a 15-drawing cycle), while a horse might lope along as slowly as 24s. A mouse, on the other hand, might scurry on 8s or even 6s.

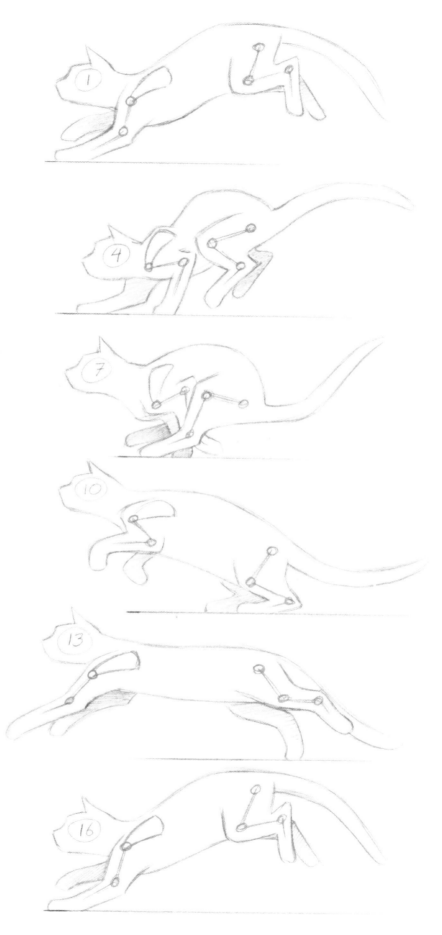

ANIMAL CHARACTER DESIGN—THE HORSE

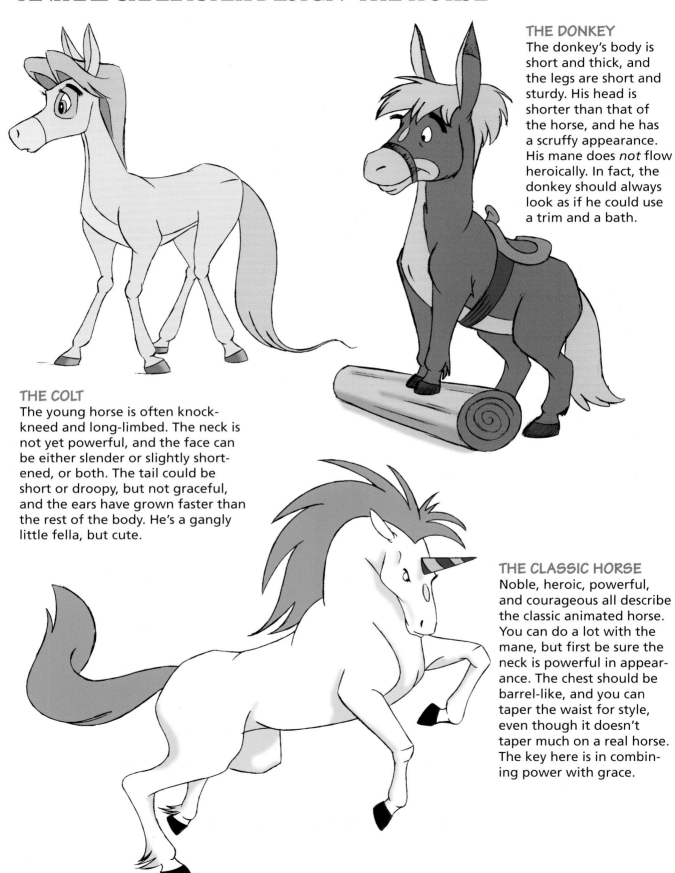

THE DONKEY
The donkey's body is short and thick, and the legs are short and sturdy. His head is shorter than that of the horse, and he has a scruffy appearance. His mane does *not* flow heroically. In fact, the donkey should always look as if he could use a trim and a bath.

THE COLT
The young horse is often knock-kneed and long-limbed. The neck is not yet powerful, and the face can be either slender or slightly short-ened, or both. The tail could be short or droopy, but not graceful, and the ears have grown faster than the rest of the body. He's a gangly little fella, but cute.

THE CLASSIC HORSE
Noble, heroic, powerful, and courageous all describe the classic animated horse. You can do a lot with the mane, but first be sure the neck is powerful in appear-ance. The chest should be barrel-like, and you can taper the waist for style, even though it doesn't taper much on a real horse. The key here is in combin-ing power with grace.

THE TRENDY HORSE

The trendy horse can be drawn with an upright, humanlike posture. It's an awkward way to draw this animal, but it's so unnatural that it becomes weirdly amusing. You can elongate the naturally long head even further. Here, the hind legs are shortened in order to make the upper body stand out, which is necessary to maintain the horse's powerful stature in this kooky pose.

ANIMAL CHARACTER DESIGN—THE BIG CAT

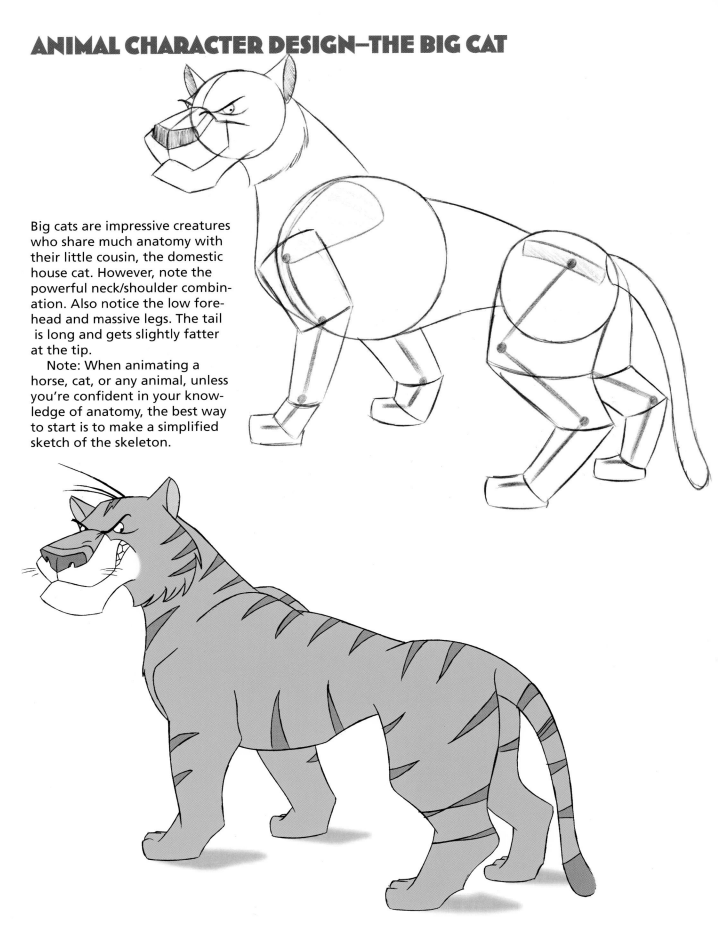

Big cats are impressive creatures who share much anatomy with their little cousin, the domestic house cat. However, note the powerful neck/shoulder combination. Also notice the low forehead and massive legs. The tail is long and gets slightly fatter at the tip.

   Note: When animating a horse, cat, or any animal, unless you're confident in your knowledge of anatomy, the best way to start is to make a simplified sketch of the skeleton.

THE GROWL

When a lion gets set to roar, its face crinkles up, allowing the victim to see the teeth *before* actually being consumed by the massive beast. I guess it's a professional courtesy or something.

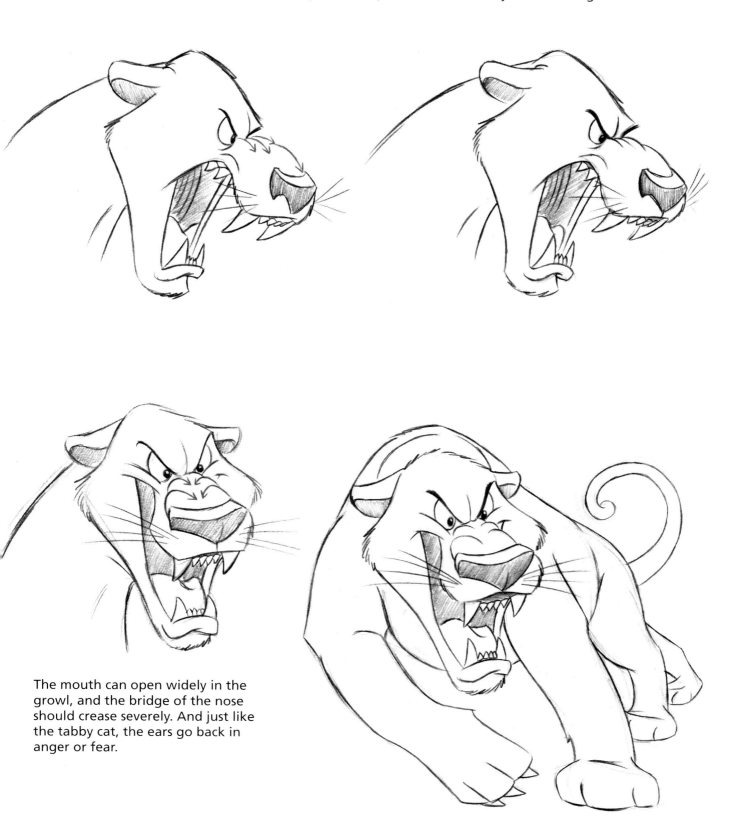

The mouth can open widely in the growl, and the bridge of the nose should crease severely. And just like the tabby cat, the ears go back in anger or fear.

THE WEDGE-SHAPED NOSE

As animation becomes more sophisticated, so does the character design. When creating a somewhat realistic cartoon animal, it's not enough to draw a black oval with a highlight on it and call it a nose. The nose must represent the type found on that particular animal. In addition, the nose must be drawn in perspective, and to do that, we must start with a solid shape that has sides (and dimension) to it.

Basic shape.

Once you have the basic shape, round it off so that it looks less mechanical.

Then draw the nostrils, with perspective added inside.

FRONT VIEW

In the front view, the bridge of the nose is severely foreshortened, due to perspective. The nose is an extension of the bridge of the nose; it isn't simply a gumball plopped on the end.

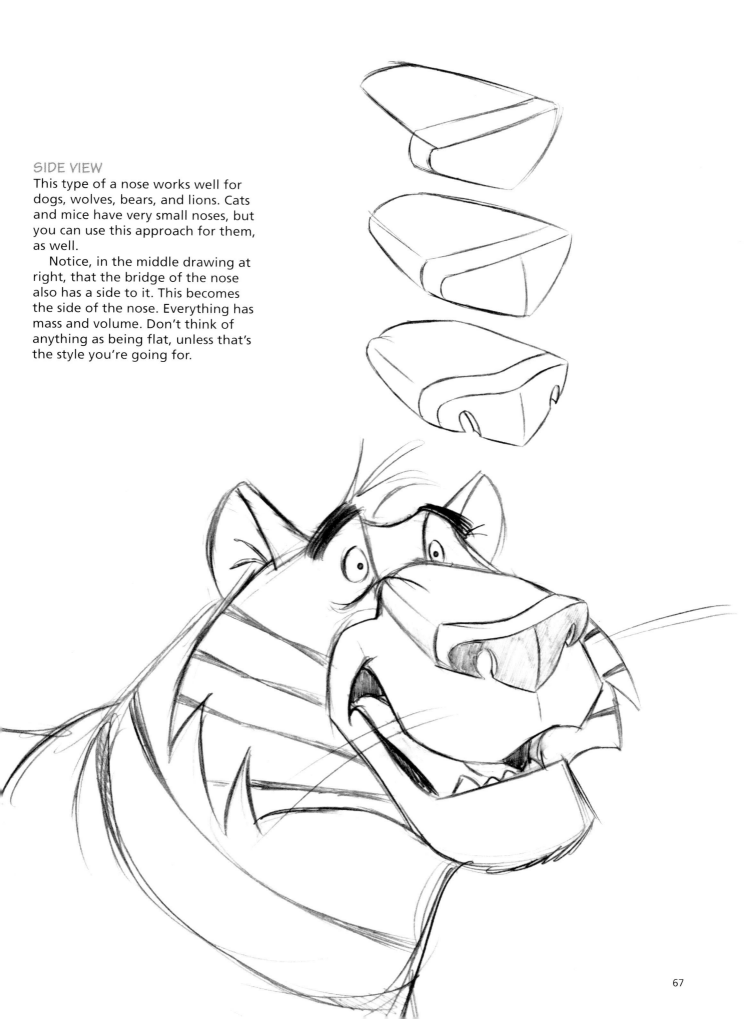

SIDE VIEW

This type of a nose works well for dogs, wolves, bears, and lions. Cats and mice have very small noses, but you can use this approach for them, as well.

Notice, in the middle drawing at right, that the bridge of the nose also has a side to it. This becomes the side of the nose. Everything has mass and volume. Don't think of anything as being flat, unless that's the style you're going for.

MARKINGS

You can make your animal characters more clearly readable and bring added focus to important parts of their faces by the effective use of markings. In addition to adding an appealing design element, the lines that connect two different colors of fur should also serve to articulate the contours of the face.

Markings primarily help to bring out the eyes and mouth of an animal. This dog has a typical arrangement of markings: The line of the lower lip rises up and curves around to become a crease line around the mouth, then continues to form the cheek, dipping below the eye and continuing along the bridge of the nose.

This pooch has enough going on in his face without additional markings, but if you wanted to, you could add markings for the eyes by forming a circle that starts at the eyebrow, travels under the eyes, and attaches back at the eyebrow again. Markings can be creative and inventive, and need not be literal representations of the markings of the animal.

SIMPLIFYING CHARACTERS FOR ANIMATION

The wolf is a popular shaggy old villain. But you'd give the other animators heart attacks if you asked them to animate every ruffle of fur for hundreds, if not thousands, of drawings. And, the producers would shoot you, because the process of drawing all that extra fur would add up to many more hours of labor and, therefore, many more dollars.

While you shouldn't edit yourself when designing a character, once you've created it, see if you can simplify the character without destroying its personality.

LABOR-INTENSIVE WOLF CHARACTER

SIMPLIFIED WOLF CHARACTER

Simplified pelvis

Less fur on back

Interior of ear doesn't have a spike of fur

Ears aren't frayed at the ends

Foot doesn't have individual footpads

Knee isn't scruffy

Tail has only one color and has fewer ruffles of fur

Chin isn't scruffy

UPRIGHT ANIMALS

It has been a long tradition in cartoons to give animals human postures. Bugs Bunny is a typical example; his legs bend the same way yours do. But there's another way to draw upright animals that's a combination of the human stance and true animal posture. Compare the examples here. The skunk has completely human posture; the knees bend just like yours or mine. The raccoon, opposite, on the other hand, retains an animal leg joint configuration, but combines this with the upright posture of a human.

Why the difference in approach? The raccoon approach is very popular in animated feature films, for which animals are generally drawn more realistically than they are for animated television shows. This posture allows the animal to resume a stance on all fours, at any time, without breaking reality.

When creating a posture for a character, also consider its personality. The raccoon character still appears to be part of the animal kingdom, even though he does some human-like things. The skunk, by contrast, appears more human due to his posture, and would be wackier. The skunk would be more likely to eat a submarine sandwich, for example, while the raccoon would look more natural nibbling on nuts or berries.

THE EVOLUTION OF A CHARACTER

When you see a well-designed character, you can be sure that it went through many stages in order to get to that point. No character starts out exactly as it ends up. There are countless changes to be made along the way, some small, some major. Basically, however, there are two types of adjustments—structural and feature.

STRUCTURAL CHANGES

These are changes in the size, shape, or form of the skull. The lengthening of a chin, lowering of a forehead, widening of a jaw, and narrowing of the back of a head are all structural changes.

FEATURE CHANGES

These adjustments are really just a matter of trial and error. If one type of nose doesn't work, try another.

These old-world characters share a similar hair style, which conveys the idea that they're from a specific period in history. However, making many small structural and feature changes results in a wide variety of totally distinct characters.

THE "BREAK OUT" DRAWING

One of the secrets of good character design is knowing when to blow the character out of the water with a totally new approach, and then reel it back in and merge that new approach with your original idea.

1

Let's say we have this oafish pirate character as a starting point but would like to create an oafish king.

2

We'll begin by adding the stereotypical king elements: a crown, an indication of a robe, a beard. At this stage, the character is pretty lame.

3

Trying to make the king more appealing by drawing small adjustments doesn't seem to be helping.

4

But now, here's the break out drawing. We lurch out in a new direction with a whole host of possibilities.

5

Finally, we tighten up the character to reveal a fairly nifty-looking king. He's far different from the first idea, yet he retains some of the original oafishness.

PUSHING PAST A USABLE DRAWING

Sometimes when creating a character, it's useful to "push past" the first acceptable drawing, in order to end up with several good final choices.

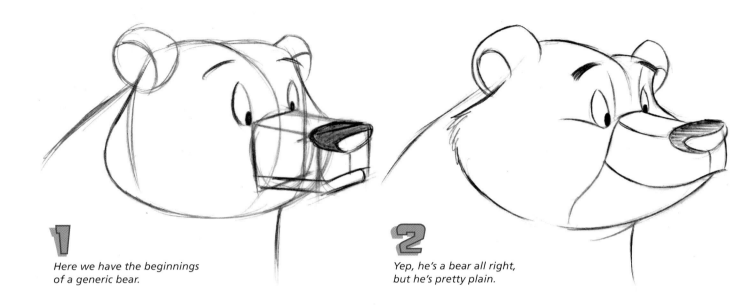

1 *Here we have the beginnings of a generic bear.*

2 *Yep, he's a bear all right, but he's pretty plain.*

3 *Here, I've shortened the chin, bunched up his cheeks, and simplified the top of his head.*

4 *By placing the ears together atop the head, the bear takes on a friendlier look. The additional eye markings also help, as do the bushier eyebrows. But, let's push on and see what happens if I go for a "break out" drawing.*

5 I wouldn't have shown this to my mom and told her that I planned to make a living drawing, but you've got to be willing to make a bad drawing in order to come up with a good one.

6 By widening the face and keeping the long snout, I have an interesting possibility.

7 Another valid bear, yet different from the first. By simply continuing the search for new forms, you can create an endless variety.

CARICATURING THE MUSCLES

The figure on the left is drawn without defining the muscles. All of the lines are straight. The figure on the right, however, shows the contours of the muscles. It looks more realistic and exudes more personality. This is another example of why life drawing is useful for the animation artist.

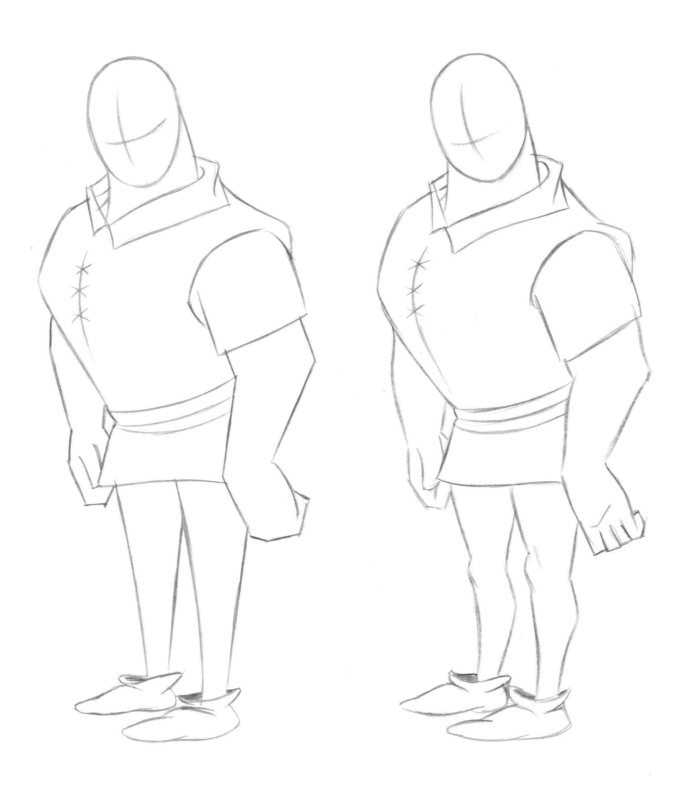

BODY SCULPTING

Think of the figure as being made of clay. You can change it any way you want, in order to create new characters. Slice away a bit here, add some more there, and . . . voilà!

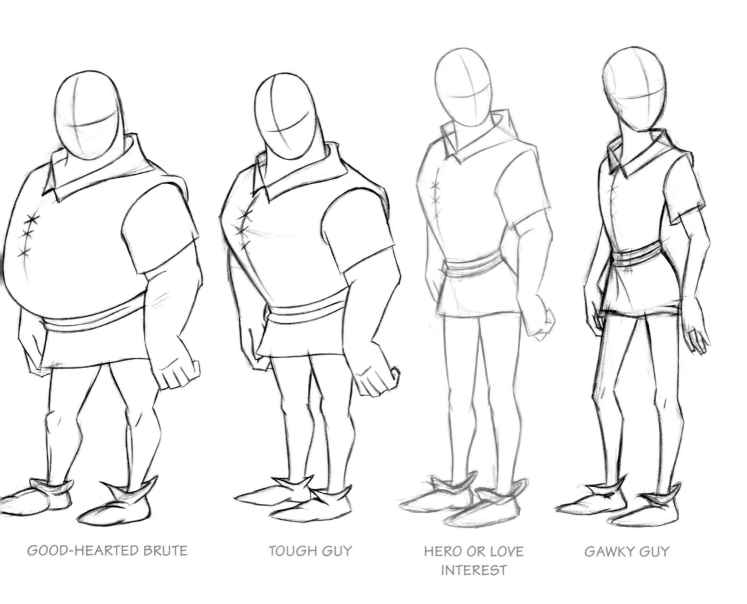

GOOD-HEARTED BRUTE

TOUGH GUY

HERO OR LOVE
INTEREST

GAWKY GUY

EXPERIMENTATION

This is the key to character design. Everything is a work-in-progress. There's an old saying that films aren't finished, they're abandoned, meaning that directors would keeping recutting and reshooting forever if the producers didn't put a stop to it.

Animation is also film. So, until you're completely satisfied—or until your producer is ready to kill you—keep plugging away.

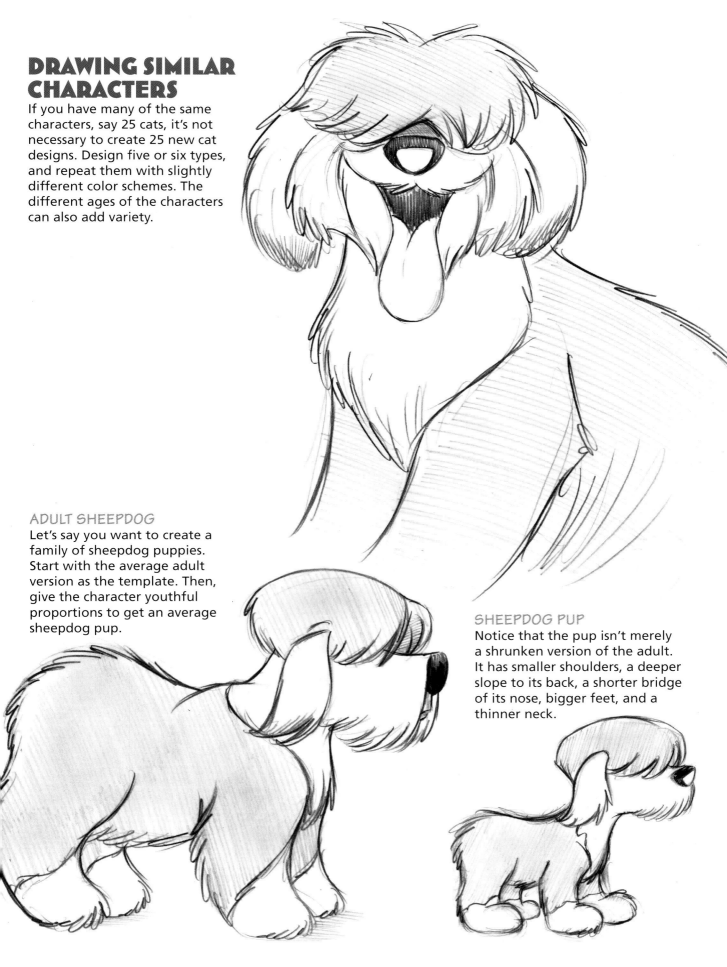

DRAWING SIMILAR CHARACTERS

If you have many of the same characters, say 25 cats, it's not necessary to create 25 new cat designs. Design five or six types, and repeat them with slightly different color schemes. The different ages of the characters can also add variety.

ADULT SHEEPDOG

Let's say you want to create a family of sheepdog puppies. Start with the average adult version as the template. Then, give the character youthful proportions to get an average sheepdog pup.

SHEEPDOG PUP

Notice that the pup isn't merely a shrunken version of the adult. It has smaller shoulders, a deeper slope to its back, a shorter bridge of its nose, bigger feet, and a thinner neck.

To create different personalities among similar animal characters, choose traits that are common to *human children,* not animals. In other words, don't use ideas like the puppy who chews the furniture or the puppy who begs to go outside. Instead, try the following:

THE CUTE GIRL

THE FAT KID

THE AFFABLE
TROUBLEMAKER

THE BRAINY KID

THE GIRL WITH THE
STYLISH HAIRDO

MODEL SHEETS

Since many people may animate the same character, a blueprint for that character is necessary. This blueprint is called the *model sheet* and it ensures that everyone is in agreement on the way the figure should look.

A model sheet should show the character's height, basic stances, quirky expressions or poses, and a variety of angles (including the mandatory front, 3/4, profile, and rear views), plus any other information necessary about how the character should be drawn.

COMPARATIVE SIZE CHARTS

Like the model sheet, the comparative size chart helps the animator stay true to the character. This size chart, from the delightful movie *Fieval Goes West,* shows all the characters lined up together so that the animators can easily judge the relative sizes of the figures.

"AMERICAN TAIL II"
SIZE COMPARISON CHART

CHARACTER TYPES

There are many "types" of cartoon characters, such as villains, heroes, cute characters, and nervous characters, among others. Within each type there are subgroups. When casting a character type, be as specific as possible in determining the subgroup. You'll get much more personality out of your character that way.

THE VILLAINOUS WOMAN

To illustrate some subgroups, I've chosen the general character type of the "villainous woman." The female villain is a wonderful type that has added humor and drama to many animated films and television shows.

THE JEALOUS SHREW

Envy and jealousy are corrosive emotions. A person dominated by them is vengeful. This character will stop at nothing to get what she wants. She may actually be able to love, albeit in a sick and possessive way. She tries to get her man by plotting to get rid of her competition—only to discover that the man she desires doesn't want her anyway.

THE SOCIALITE

She loves to entertain and has no true feelings for anyone but herself. She's fiercely competitive and a tyrant to work for.

THE WICKED STEPMOTHER

This type's a classic. She should look more like a grandmother than a mother. Nothing about her should be cuddly. She can never be redeemed. She has sharp features, flared nostrils, thin eyebrows, and tight lips. While I assume real stepmothers are by and large a kind and loving group, in animation, they're not.

RICH AND EVIL
They say that by the time you're 50, you get the face you deserve. And this lady has got it! It's a sharp, pinched face, incapable of soft expressions. The angular cheekbones and ultra-thin eyebrows highlight the character's razor-sharp qualities. Even the body stands rigidly.

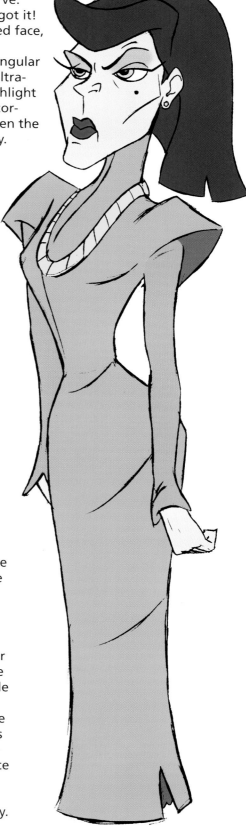

THE ICE LADY
This popular type of female villain is as beautiful as she is cold. She's only out for herself. She may possess some magical powers, or she may be an incarnation of some demonic form. Her eyes are hypnotic and have the power to charm gullible men—and even men of power. Heavy eyelids are effective for evil characters of any gender. Note the high cheekbones. And, note how placid the face is, as if the facade of beauty is covering up something ugly.

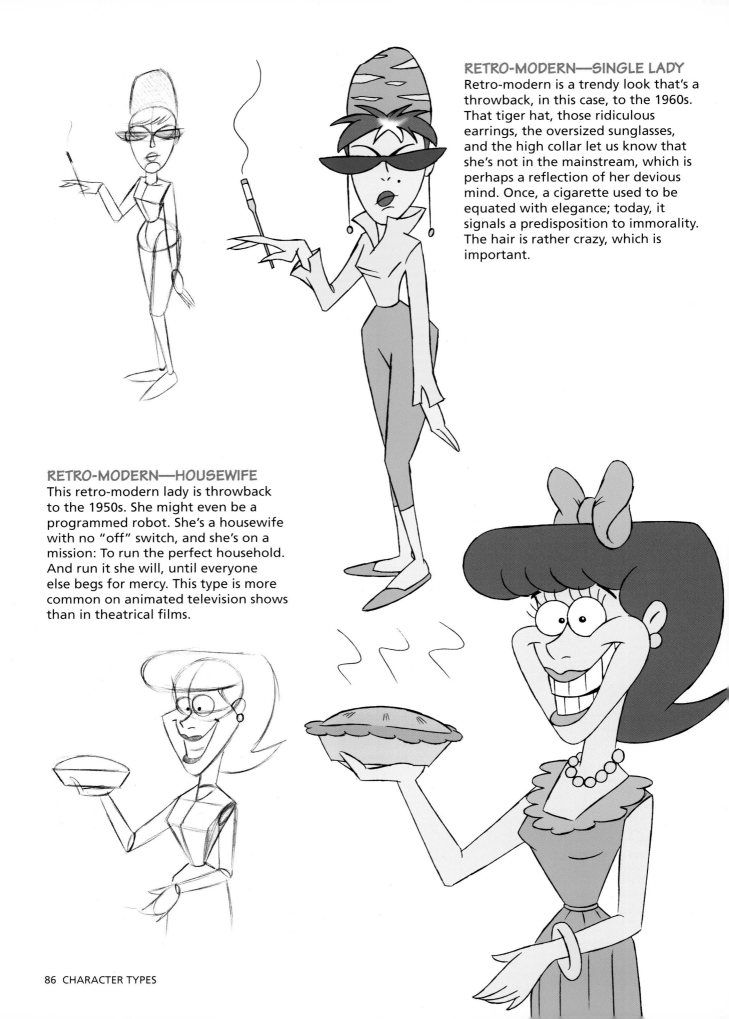

RETRO-MODERN—SINGLE LADY

Retro-modern is a trendy look that's a throwback, in this case, to the 1960s. That tiger hat, those ridiculous earrings, the oversized sunglasses, and the high collar let us know that she's not in the mainstream, which is perhaps a reflection of her devious mind. Once, a cigarette used to be equated with elegance; today, it signals a predisposition to immorality. The hair is rather crazy, which is important.

RETRO-MODERN—HOUSEWIFE

This retro-modern lady is throwback to the 1950s. She might even be a programmed robot. She's a housewife with no "off" switch, and she's on a mission: To run the perfect household. And run it she will, until everyone else begs for mercy. This type is more common on animated television shows than in theatrical films.

MODERN WITCH

Not every witch needs to be of the Hansel-and-Gretel variety. There are good looking witches, and fat, cuddly ones, too. Any evil woman with a book of magic spells and a cauldron can be a witch. She doesn't need a stovepipe hat and a broomstick. Rather than abandoning a character type like the witch because it's too old fashioned for your story, try to reinvent the character in a modern way. Witches typically delight in their evil, so you should design their faces with broad smiles in mind. They're eccentric bad girls, so give them sloppy hairdos. And, have fun with them.

FATHERS

Try to design your characters, in this case fathers, to fit very specific stereotype categories. The more specific you are when creating your characters, the easier it will be for the story writers to come up with crisp, appropriate dialogue for them, because the characters will convey a clear point of view.

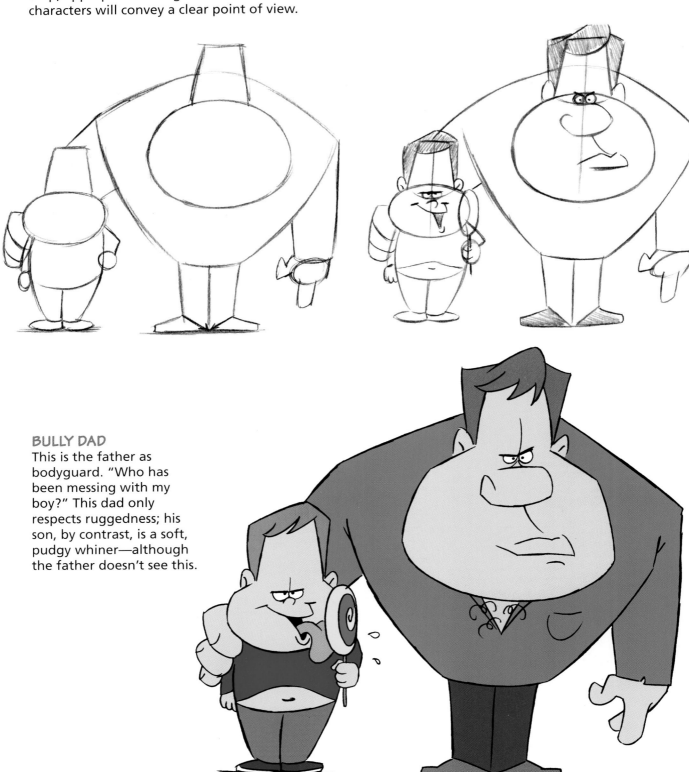

BULLY DAD

This is the father as bodyguard. "Who has been messing with my boy?" This dad only respects ruggedness; his son, by contrast, is a soft, pudgy whiner—although the father doesn't see this.

RETRO DAD

This is the father who still thinks corporate America is the working man's best friend. He believes in goodness, ethics, and the American way. He used to be cast as the hero in sitcoms of the early 1960s but is now seen as a weird, almost manic dad whose "golly gee" manner hides a darker, albeit humorous, side.

YOUNG DAD

This father's in a little over his head in the child rearing department. He's not a strict disciplinarian, either. Good-natured, though a beat behind, he's a "sensitive" dad, who shares the household chores with his wife.

COUCH POTATO DAD

We all know this guy. In fact, some of us *are* this guy. He's the epitome of middle class values: work at a job you hate, come home to a wife whose problems you'd rather ignore, and hide from the children before they beg you for spending money.

HOW TO DRAW CHILDREN

f you look at medieval paintings, you'll find that the artists didn't know how to paint children. They painted them as if they were tiny adults, with adult proportions. You need to know what makes kids different from adults in order to exaggerate those qualities and create successful child characters.

Babies and toddlers are adorable, but since they don't do very much except eat, drool, walk, and fall, they're not typically the stars of animated films. However, older children are. I've broken them down into two categories, as their physical properties differ with age.

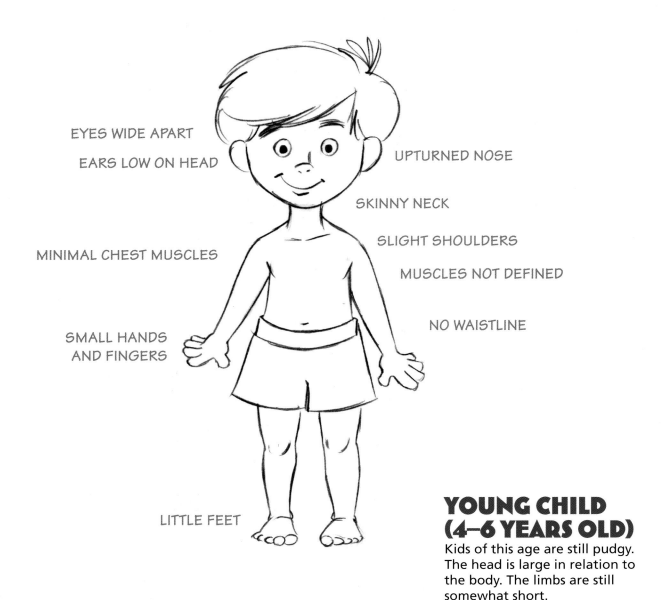

EYES WIDE APART

EARS LOW ON HEAD

UPTURNED NOSE

SKINNY NECK

SLIGHT SHOULDERS

MINIMAL CHEST MUSCLES

MUSCLES NOT DEFINED

NO WAISTLINE

SMALL HANDS
AND FINGERS

LITTLE FEET

YOUNG CHILD (4–6 YEARS OLD)
Kids of this age are still pudgy. The head is large in relation to the body. The limbs are still somewhat short.

OLDER KID (7–10 YEARS OLD)

Children of this age group have longer limbs, which can be a bit gangly. Their baby fat has disappeared, and the head is smaller in comparison to the size of the body.

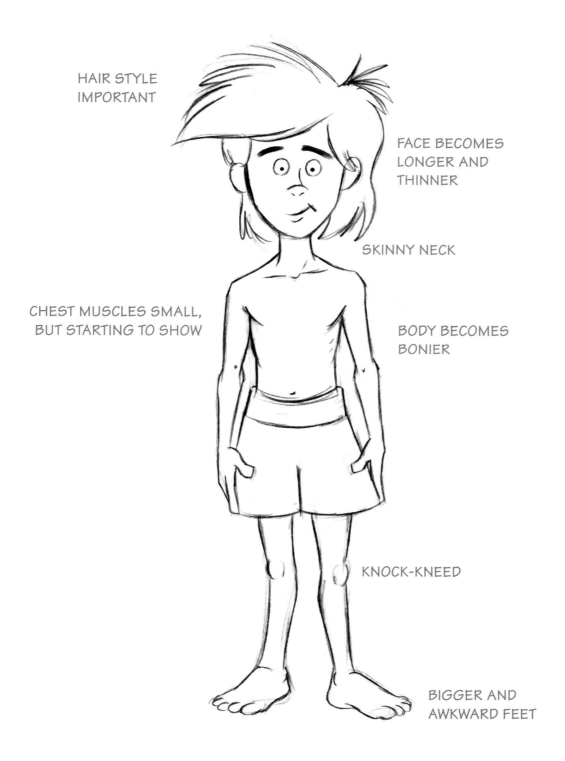

HAIR STYLE IMPORTANT

FACE BECOMES LONGER AND THINNER

SKINNY NECK

CHEST MUSCLES SMALL, BUT STARTING TO SHOW

BODY BECOMES BONIER

KNOCK-KNEED

BIGGER AND AWKWARD FEET

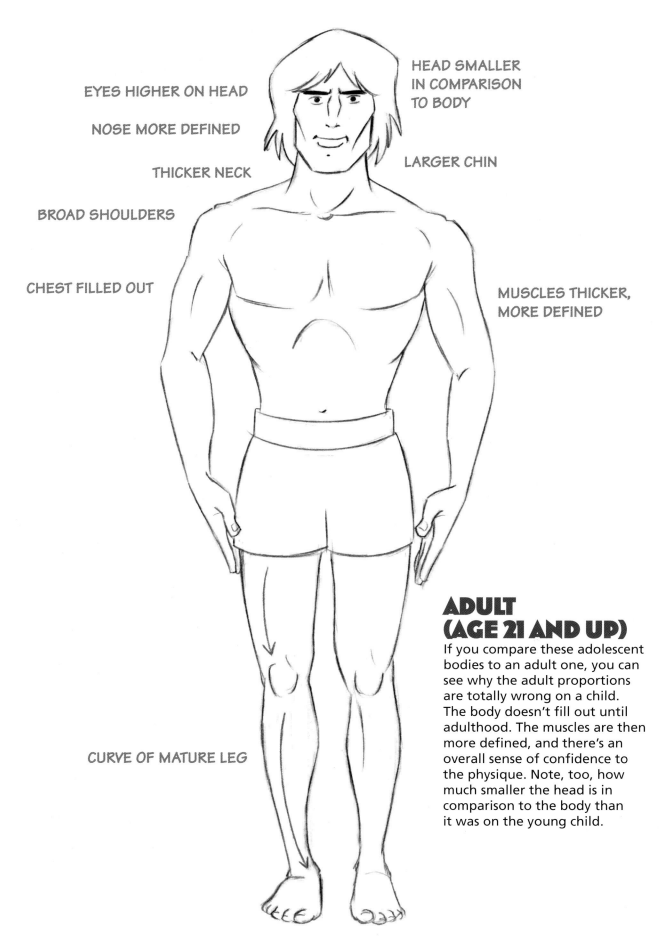

EYES HIGHER ON HEAD

NOSE MORE DEFINED

THICKER NECK

BROAD SHOULDERS

CHEST FILLED OUT

HEAD SMALLER
IN COMPARISON
TO BODY

LARGER CHIN

MUSCLES THICKER,
MORE DEFINED

CURVE OF MATURE LEG

ADULT (AGE 21 AND UP)

If you compare these adolescent bodies to an adult one, you can see why the adult proportions are totally wrong on a child. The body doesn't fill out until adulthood. The muscles are then more defined, and there's an overall sense of confidence to the physique. Note, too, how much smaller the head is in comparison to the body than it was on the young child.

TYPES OF KIDS

Kids come in all different sizes, body types, and personalities. In general, though, keep the head large. Unless the character is wacky, cute little hands and feet are best until the kid starts to get a little older and become gangly. Never give a kid wide shoulders, unless he or she is a bully.

Upturned noses are the most common, and the younger the child is, the smaller the nose will be. Place the ears low down on the face; the younger the child, the lower the ears. Eyes can be wide and large, *but they don't have to be.*

Vary the hair styles. Kids have lots of hair, and the way they choose to grow and comb it reflects their identity. Also, don't assume that fat kids should always be cuddly; they can be obnoxious, just like the rest of us!

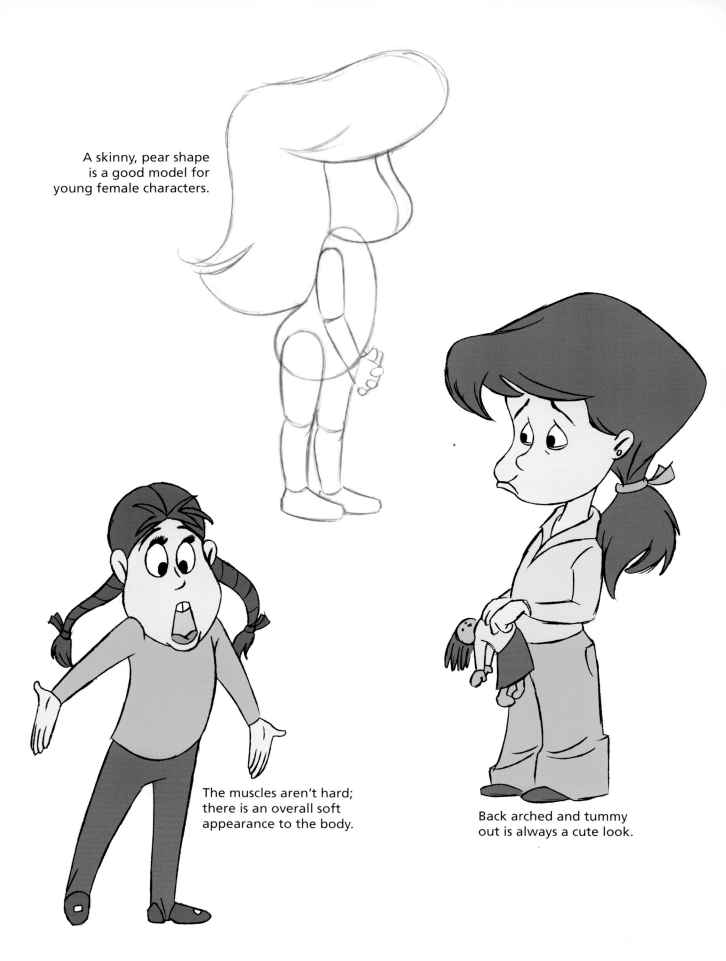

A skinny, pear shape is a good model for young female characters.

The muscles aren't hard; there is an overall soft appearance to the body.

Back arched and tummy out is always a cute look.

Sports items make good props for kids, who always seem to be on their way to or from a game.

Young characters should convey unbridled energy. Girls aren't always reserved, peaches-and-cream types—they can compete with the boys on an equal footing.

Go with the latest trends, including hairstyles. But don't go for anything truly antisocial, otherwise your character will lose its appeal. Parents will shun it, as will sponsors.

COSTUME DESIGN

TODAY'S MAN
The emphasis is on functional clothing.

Films that are set in a past time in history are known as "period pieces." You can quickly recognize them, for example, by their vintage automobiles, furniture, and "shoppes." This is the territory of the background and layout artists, who we'll get to on page 130. But the animator does have to be concerned with the costumes.

In live action features, the expense of locating vintage cars and building antique sets is enormous, but with animation, it's no more expensive to draw a 19th-century townhouse than it is to draw a modern one. There's just more research involved. Libraries, museums, and old and period-piece movies are all great sources for information on historical styles.

Animated period pieces have artistic advantages, as well. They place the story in a dreamy setting, which instantly invokes the feeling of a "classic." The audience looks at period pieces with curiosity, like a window to the past. Plus, the designs of the past are more ornate, and therefore, period piece films tend to look very pretty. In fact, in the past, men were typically dressed in costumes that were just as elaborate as those worn by women.

We also associate the past with innocence and charm, which is conducive to the plots of many animated tales. There were also stronger social boundaries in the past, and that creates a setting for good drama.

PERIOD PIECE MAN
Flamboyant clothing was the norm for men—lots of layers, buttons, and powdered wigs.

96

TODAY'S WOMAN
The emphasis is on body hugging, clingy, and revealing clothes. Her hair has that conspicuously careless look. She wants to stand out.

PERIOD PIECE WOMAN
Her makeup isn't severe. Her hair style is conventional. Her eyes are large, conveying a sense of innocence. She's feminine, but not weak—remember, life was hard back then. Features are classic, rather than eclectic.

1800s—FRANCE

There are many periods in history, from Roman to Medieval to Viking, and so on. Obviously, there isn't enough room to cover them all here. Therefore, I thought it would be most instructive to consider the clothes from a few small segments of the more recent past, in which we can easily see the roots of our current fashions.

The French were probably the most flamboyant dressers, with the most opulent fabrics. They wore ruffled sleeves, and wigs for both men and women. Men wore knicker-type pants and tights with slipper-like shoes that had buckles on them. Handkerchiefs were a common accessory. Women wore dresses that narrowed drastically at the waist and then expanded in a wide oval, and draped down to the floor. Fans were common accessories for women.

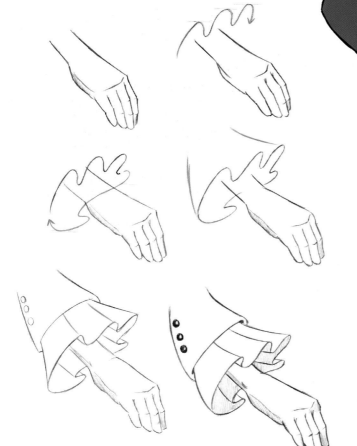

RUFFLES

The ruffles should overlap to get the best look. Draw the interior and exterior of the overlaps, and remember that, on shirts, the sleeves widened out at the ends.

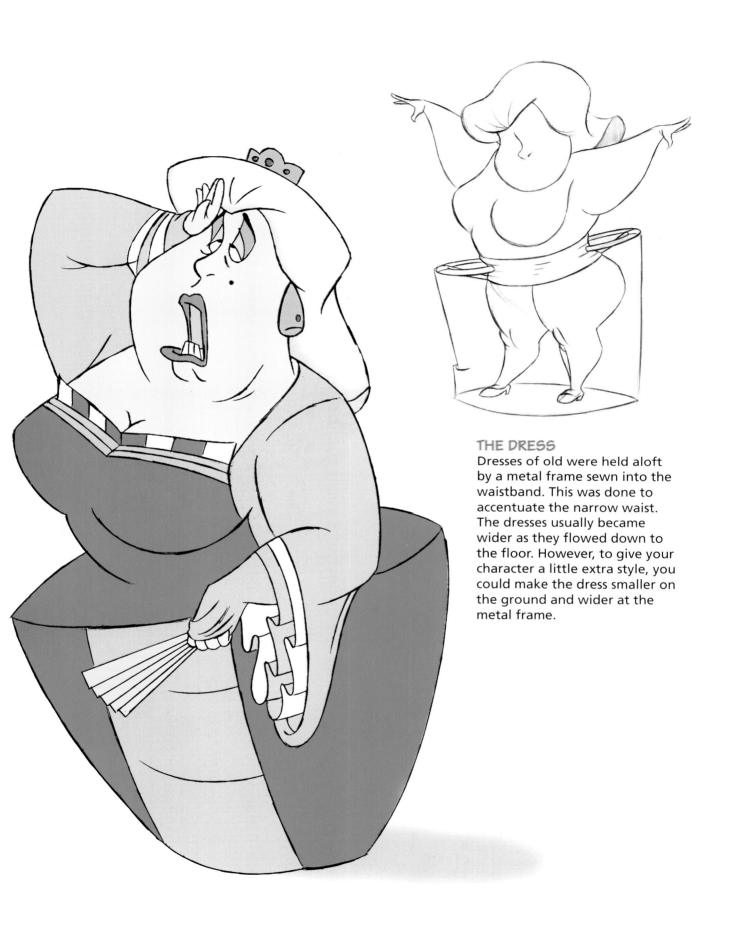

THE DRESS
Dresses of old were held aloft by a metal frame sewn into the waistband. This was done to accentuate the narrow waist. The dresses usually became wider as they flowed down to the floor. However, to give your character a little extra style, you could make the dress smaller on the ground and wider at the metal frame.

EARLY 1800s—AMERICA

Although the American wardrobe of the 1800s had many layers, it was completely different from that of the French. American costumes have a "proper," Puritan feel to them. They were no-nonsense. (Think of schoolmarms and bankers.) They were similar to the English, Dickensian style. The bonnet, top hat, shawl, and vest were common. Oversized mutton sleeves (puffy from shoulder to elbow and fitted from elbow to wrist) on ladies were typical of that era.

THE GLOVE
Gloves with cut-outs for the fingers were popular. Who thought this was a good idea?

LATE 1800s—AMERICA

By the 1890s, American clothes had begun to look more like today's modern counterparts, although everything was more formal. Hats for men were common, as they were for ladies. Ties were worn by both genders, as well. In fact, the clothing had a strange symmetry between men and women. Note the high collar of the man's shirt and the pocket configuration on the jacket. Pant and shirt cuffs were oversized, and there was still a bit of flourish on women's sleeves.

CHILDREN—LATE 1800s, AMERICA

Children were dressed properly in little outfits. Sailor outfits were popular turn-of-the-century clothes for kids. Note that the girl (left) wears an oversized belt and boots without laces, while the boy wears no visible belt and laced boots. The collars flop over the shoulders.

Children's day-to-day clothing could be looser and freer than that of adults. And remember, they didn't have sneakers back then!

MOTORISTS—EARLY 1900s, AMERICA

Cars were new at this time, and motoring was all the rage. Driving was the thing to do, and with this, came motoring fashions. Goggles (early automobiles had no windshields), gloves, caps, and scarves were worn. Everyone was decked out to zoom along at a swift 12 miles per hour on bumpy dirt roads.

   Note the tie-down of the woman's cap and the extra material that drapes over her shoulders. The man's coat is thick, as are the flaps over his sleeve cuffs. Umbrellas were a common accessory. A double-breasted button pattern on both men's and women's coats was popular, as well.

STYLIZING A PERIOD CHARACTER

Don't be afraid to use a modern stylistic approach when creating a historical character. The audience likes to look back on the past, but does so with modern eyes. To be entertaining, your animation still has to be cutting edge, even if it's of another era. Note the various stylized elements of this period character's anatomy:

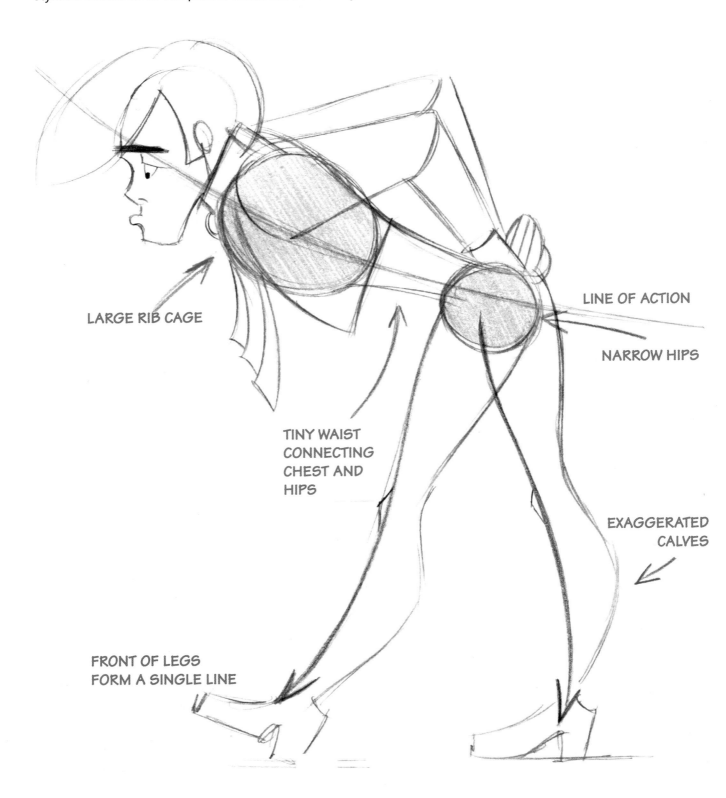

LARGE RIB CAGE

LINE OF ACTION

NARROW HIPS

TINY WAIST
CONNECTING
CHEST AND
HIPS

EXAGGERATED
CALVES

FRONT OF LEGS
FORM A SINGLE LINE

PERIOD COSTUME INVENTION

After you familiarize yourself with costumes of a particular era, you can create your own variations from your imagination. Of course, you don't want to create a character who wears a few items from the 16th century, some from the 17th, and a couple from the 20th. However, if you stay relatively within the boundaries of what was being worn at a particular time, you'll be okay.

This character's costume is a total invention, but it is simple enough and derivative enough to look reasonably authentic. I would cast him somewhere in the 1800s.

ANIMATION TECHNIQUES

We've already covered a good deal of animation techniques, from basics, like squash and stretch, to more advanced theories of action, like the realistic human walk and animal gates. This chapter covers more techniques that are a working part of the animator's vocabulary.

DISTORTION, SMEAR, AND BLUR

Mr. Basic (right) will make the "smear" pretty simple. Just take two extreme poses that are far apart, and use a distorted image of the character to fill the space between the two extremes. The distortion is then used as a huge in-between. Here, drawings 3 and 5 are the extremes, and drawing 4—the distortion—is the in-between.

One hint: Draw the distortion along the "arc" of the action. This simply means that the action between one extreme and another is not merely going in a straight line, but curving along an arc. You can see here that drawing 4 takes up the space between drawings 3 and 5 along the same arc, sloping backward.

Go for rubbery, zippy action. This bit contains both stretched out distortion in-betweens and multiple images (extra hands, feet, or legs to indicate motion and speed). Multiple images and blurs of running feet can be used to wonderfully zany effect.

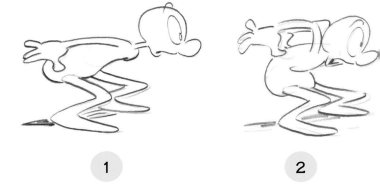

1

2

6

7

8

3

4

5

9

10

SLOW-IN, SLOW-OUT

In order to keep your animation visually interesting, you've got to vary the pace at which a character moves. I'm sure you've seen animated television shows in which all the characters move at the same, languid pace; it looks like they're walking through molasses. The problem is in the timing. Normally, a motion starts off slowly, picks up speed, and then slows down again before stopping. This principle is called *slow-in, slow-out.* Mr. Basic's cat below will demonstrate: Figures 1, 4, and 8 are the extremes. The animator adds notations to the extremes to show how the drawings should be spaced. In the notation on figure 4, for example, we can see that the animator wants figure 2 to be very close in position to figure 1, as the character *slows out* of the anticipatory pose. The animator's notation indicates that figure 3 should be spaced further away, as the action picks up speed. (The "x" indicates a beat, not a drawing.) Figure 4 is much farther from figure 3 and represents a sudden move.

Remember the following rule: The faster the action, the fewer the drawings; the slower the action, the more drawings.

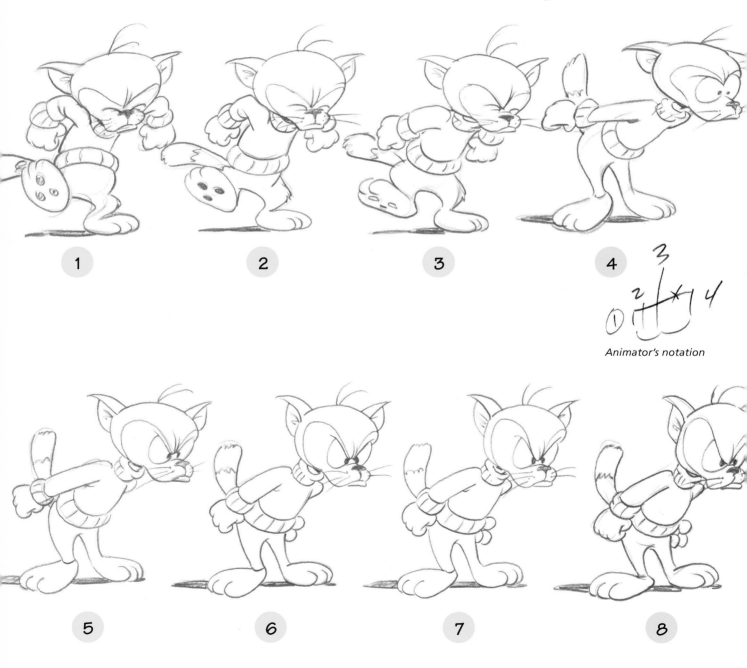

Animator's notation

THE SETTLE

When a character strikes a pose, it must settle into the action or it will look as if it has been zapped by a ray gun and frozen stiff. This is how Mr. Basic settles: He slows out of drawing 4 to settle into the final, held pose, drawing 7.

1

2

3

4

5

6

7

FORCED PERSPECTIVE

You can use forced perspective to register an extreme reaction, or to emphasize an action such as a punch or a kick. To force the perspective, push the character either toward or away from the camera. Drawings 1 and 2 here are the anticipation. Drawing 3 is the in-between. Drawing 4 is the final pose, which needs to be settled into.

1

2

3

4

THE CARTOON TAKE

Mr. Basic can't believe his ears! Of course, he doesn't have any ears, but anyway. . . .The *cartoon take* (a strong reaction) is a staple of animation. Not every take is as extreme as this one—and some are even wilder—but they all have the same components: anticipation, reaction, settle.

Don't be afraid to really stretch and distort your character during the take. Animation generally requires 12 drawings per second, so a distorted drawing will only be on the screen for a very short time before the character settles back to normal.

In this example, drawings 1 through 4 show *big* anticipation. Drawings 5 and 6 are distorted drawings that zip into drawing 7. Drawing 8 is the settling pose in which Mr. Basic regains his original form.

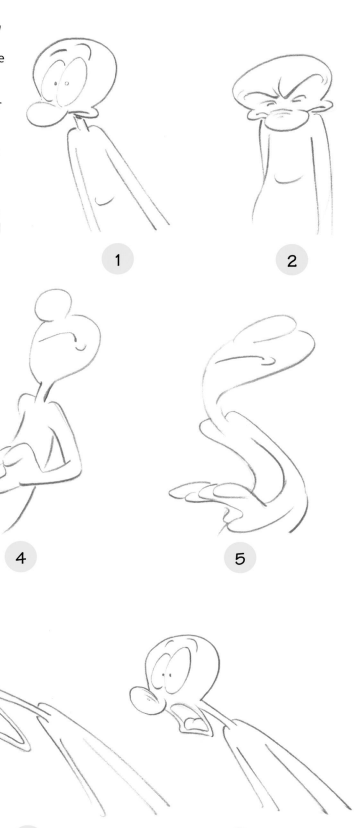

1

2

3

4

5

6

7

8

THE DOUBLE TAKE AND HEAD TURNS

Any *take* is a strong reaction. A *double take* is used mostly when a character is completely baffled, as if he's shaking his head in order to get it all straight before he takes a second look. Notice that in this double take, the dog turns his head three times before he reacts. Note, too, the drag of the jowls and ears as they lag a beat behind the action.

Whether characters do takes, or just turn casually to look at something, the head generally dips first, then arcs back up.

1

WRONG

Head stays on same plane as it turns from side to side.

RIGHT

Head dips as it turns from side to side.

6

10

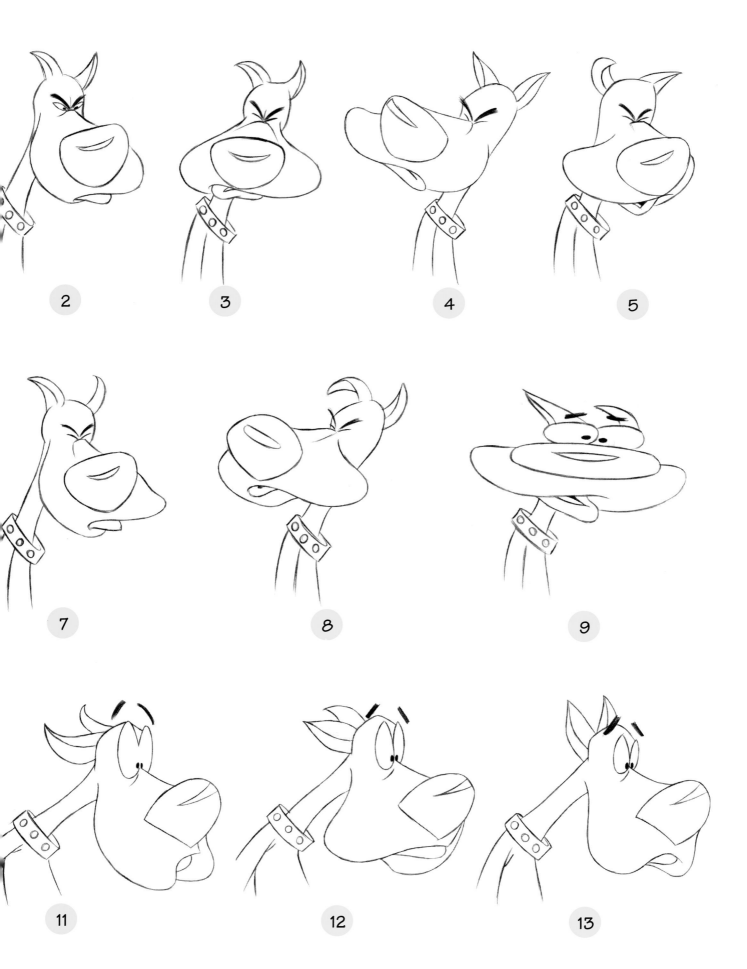

2

3

4

5

7

8

9

11

12

13

TANGENTS

Tangents are intersecting lines, which flatten out your drawings. They make items that may be widely separated seem to be on the same level. Avoiding tangents is one of the secrets of quality animation. While tangents are sometimes used deliberately in illustration, they're emphatically avoided in animation.

Animated characters are two dimensional and, therefore, flat. Animators take great pains to draw them so that they appear round and three dimensional. But, if a line in one character touches a line in another character (or object in the frame), suddenly the illusion of three-dimensionality is broken, and the characters look like the flat drawings that they really are.

Consider the example here. The man with the horn is standing behind the woman. But, when his horn touches her dress, creating tangents, he suddenly looks like he's on the same plane with her. You can see tangent points on the woman's hat and hands where they intersect with the background.

As the drawing is now, the trumpeter seems to be a "fresh" little man. Positioning him just a little higher on the background, and making sure he doesn't touch the woman's dress, would give the correct impression that he's standing behind the woman. Carefully compose your shots so that the characters work well with each other and with the backgrounds.

Here are a few more examples of how tangents make a drawing go flat. By carefully planning your poses, you can avoid mistakes like these and make your scenes work in three dimensions.

This man appears to have his nose stuck to a very small door. (The door also forms a tangent with the edge of the picture plane.) He's also standing well below the floor level.

Here, the door has been moved away from the edge of the picture plane, and the man's nose projects over it so that he now appears to be balancing the doorknob on his nose. He's also still standing well below floor level.

Tangents can be very common in the individual animated characters themselves. There are 11 tangents on this pig. Can you find them? Also, the eyes are an exception to the "no touching the lines" rule. Lines there can touch one another, and the pupils should only be surrounded by white if the character is acting scared, manic, or enraged.

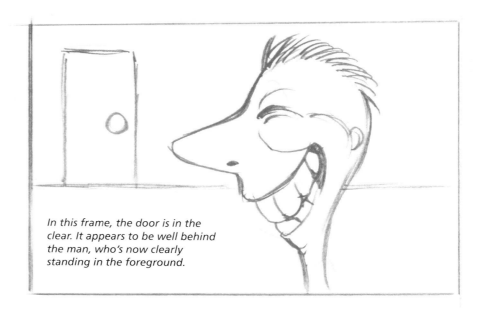

In this frame, the door is in the clear. It appears to be well behind the man, who's now clearly standing in the foreground.

OVERLAPPING ACTION

One of the most important things to remember in animation is this: By *not* having all the parts of a character's body move at the same speed, you'll give a feeling of solidity and weight to your drawings. This is referred to as *overlapping action* .

Here, in the first four drawings, the beaver leads with its head. The tail, moving differently, accentuates the line of action. In the fifth and sixth drawings, the beaver leads with its left foot. Note the arcs on the head, arms, tail, and belly; they all move at different rates, with the tail having the most rapid movement. The arms can flail around between the fourth and fifth drawings, but essentially move in a circle.

There are times when you'll have similar characters doing similar things and neither of them will be leading. In those instances, go for pleasing composition.

Notice how the line of action can work through both of the dancing pigs.

The bossy pig is leading in this scene.

SYMMETRY AND "TWINNING"

Avoid symmetry, or "twinning." These little piggies are the same size and shape. In situations like this, when there's no variety in character design, work for strong poses. Find your lead character, which will be your center of interest, and call attention to it through staging.

Avoid symmetry. Here, the facial expressions and the position of the ears have been varied. Although the heads are nearly identical in size, symmetry is avoided with staging.

POSITIONING YOUR CHARACTERS

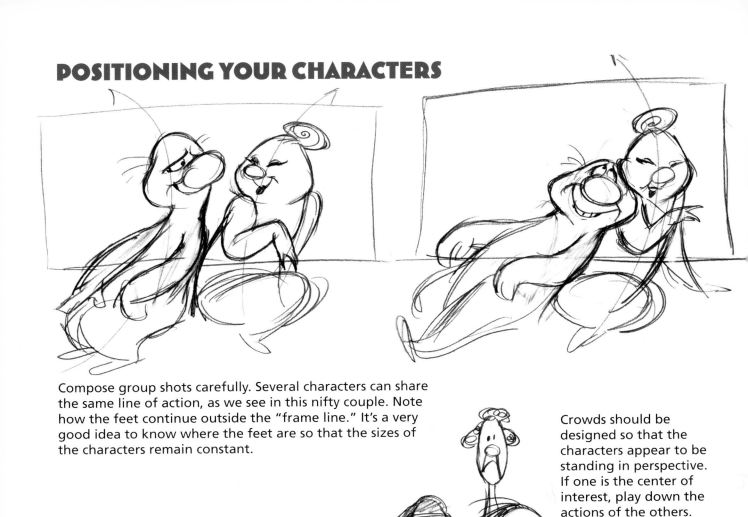

Compose group shots carefully. Several characters can share the same line of action, as we see in this nifty couple. Note how the feet continue outside the "frame line." It's a very good idea to know where the feet are so that the sizes of the characters remain constant.

Crowds should be designed so that the characters appear to be standing in perspective. If one is the center of interest, play down the actions of the others.

Silhouette shots are the easiest to read. Noses and props can point to the center of interest even better than a finger can. The audience should look where you want them to.

Your center of interest doesn't always have to be in the foreground. Since the larger, foremost pig is fairly still, while the two smaller ones are more animated, he doesn't hog the audience's interest, even though he fills the frame.

ANIMATING TWO OR MORE CHARACTERS IN A SCENE

When working with multiple characters, work for contrast in size and shape. Here, the thin figure leads in drawings 1 and 2. In 3, the fat one takes over, and the center of interest shifts to the right. Note how the lines of action complement each other and change when necessary. Timing isn't indicated, since each character would move at a different rate.

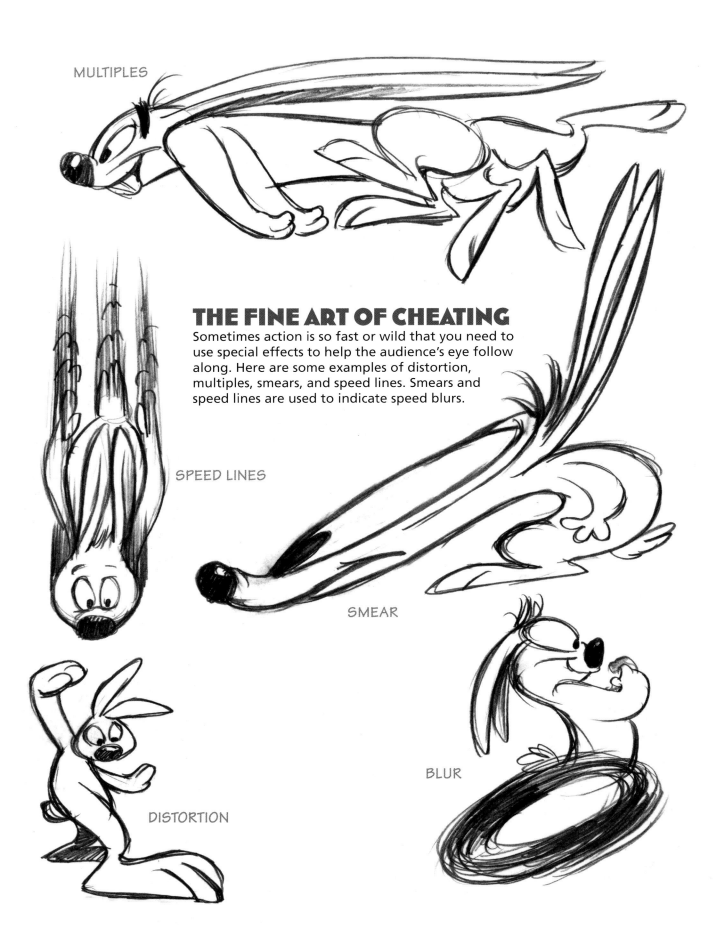

MULTIPLES

THE FINE ART OF CHEATING

Sometimes action is so fast or wild that you need to use special effects to help the audience's eye follow along. Here are some examples of distortion, multiples, smears, and speed lines. Smears and speed lines are used to indicate speed blurs.

SPEED LINES

SMEAR

BLUR

DISTORTION

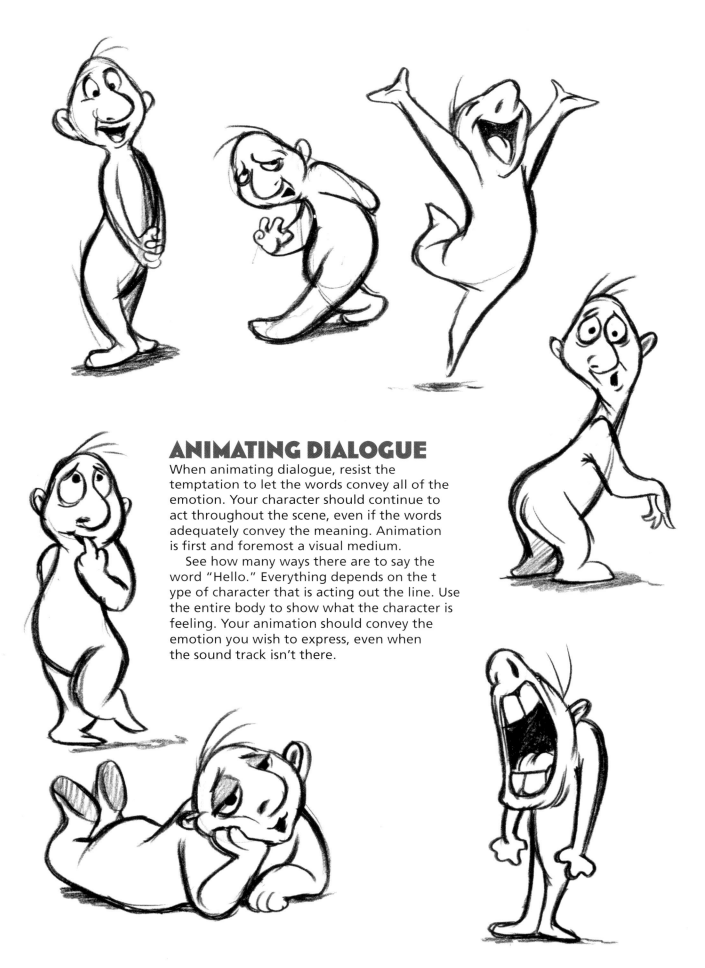

ANIMATING DIALOGUE

When animating dialogue, resist the temptation to let the words convey all of the emotion. Your character should continue to act throughout the scene, even if the words adequately convey the meaning. Animation is first and foremost a visual medium.

See how many ways there are to say the word "Hello." Everything depends on the t ype of character that is acting out the line. Use the entire body to show what the character is feeling. Your animation should convey the emotion you wish to express, even when the sound track isn't there.

SOUNDING OUT WORDS

It's not what you say, it's how you say it. No two characters will say a line the same way; they can have physical differences that will affect the way they move their mouths. See how the mouth changes when a simple word is said by a man, a horse, and a bird.

Think phonetically. Don't literally articulate every letter unless it's called for. Sometimes a few letters in a word are bunched together; the word "probably" might be spoken as "probbly," with only two syllables.

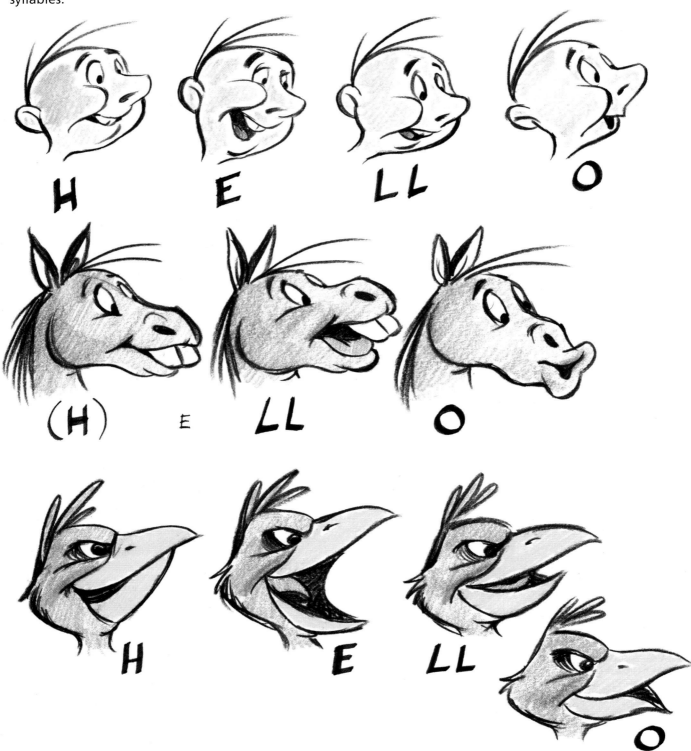

ACTING AND DIALOGUE

Consider the character's entire body when animating dialogue. Here, the pigs say the same line in two very different ways. The top pig tries to remember how to pronounce the word; he rotates his torso to show indecisiveness and displays relief at the end by relaxing the tension in his body and ears. The bottom pig has been watching too many horror movies and knows exactly how to say the word; his body remains in the same basic pose throughout and the acting becomes more focused. Always think about how your characters feel and have their actions express their inner thoughts.

TECHNICAL STUFF

READING THE EXPOSURE SHEET

Dialogue is recorded before the animator begins to animate it. The sounds and pauses of the dialogue are written out frame by frame on an *exposure sheet,* and the animator follows it so that the drawings will match up with the correct sounds.

Take a look at the exposure sheet at right. The heading "Dial" means *dialogue* and counts off the frame numbers for each piece of dialogue. The dialogue itself is written down phonetically, for the corresponding frames, under the column "Track," which stands for *dialogue soundtrack.*

The "A" and "B" notations stand for the cel levels, in this case two—A level and B level. Each character is drawn on a separate cel level. A cel is a piece of acetate that is placed over a pencil animation drawing, then inked and painted, thereby allowing the background to show through it. Many studios avoid inking and painting by scanning the pencil drawings directly into the computer, where they're inked and painted digitally.

When layering film under the camera, the background is placed down first. The A level cel goes on top of that, then the B level goes on top of that, then the C level, and so on, depending on how many characters you have. The next three columns in the chart indicate this order.

An "x" mark in these columns indicates a blank cel, which is used to keep colors constant. For example, if you have two cels and suddenly add a third, the colors will become duller when

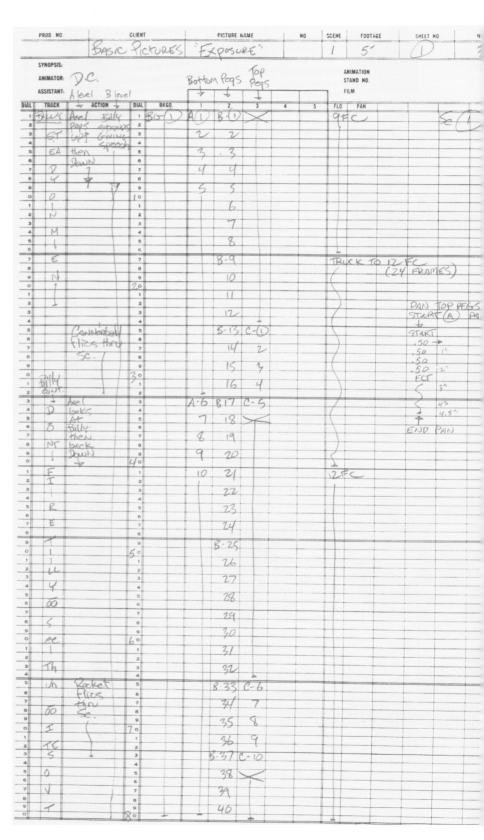

you pile this third layer of acetate onto it. To prevent this color change, you put a blank cel on the first two cels (for the frames in which there is no third cel). Then, when you add the third character cel, you replace the blank cel with a character cel; there's no change in value, since the number of layers of acetate remains constant throughout the process.

In the column hand-labeled "Bottom" (meaning bottom cel), A5 is a held cel. This means that the character isn't being animated for those frames up until A6, perhaps because he has stopped to pause.

In the "FLD" column, the notation "FC" stands for *field calibrations,* which indicates that the action moves from one field (area of the artwork) to another. To go to a larger field, you *truck out.* Trucking out means that the camera pulls back from the art, allowing more of it to be seen and resulting in a larger field. So, going from a 9FC to a 12FC, as indicated in this column, is a truck out. Going from a 12FC to a 9FC would be a *truck in.*

THE ANIMATION CAMERA

This is a typical set up for an Oxberry animation camera. The camera can move up and down (truck in and out) but not side to side; the artwork moves from side to side. The glass platen presses down on the cels before the frames are clicked off to keep the artwork smooth.

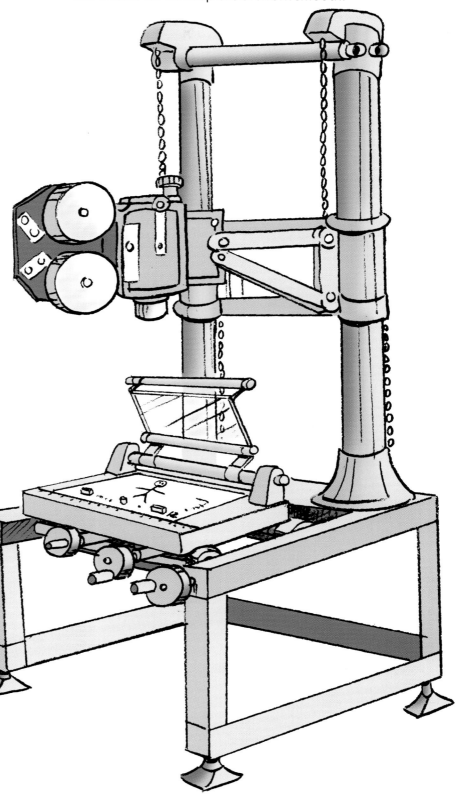

THE FIELD GUIDE

This is a "map" of the area of the artwork that gives the cameraperson specific instructions on where the art should be moved and by how much. You can see by looking at it that a size 4 field is much smaller than a size 9 field. The artwork can be moved in four directions —north, east, south and west, as indicated by the direction letters N, E, S, and W.

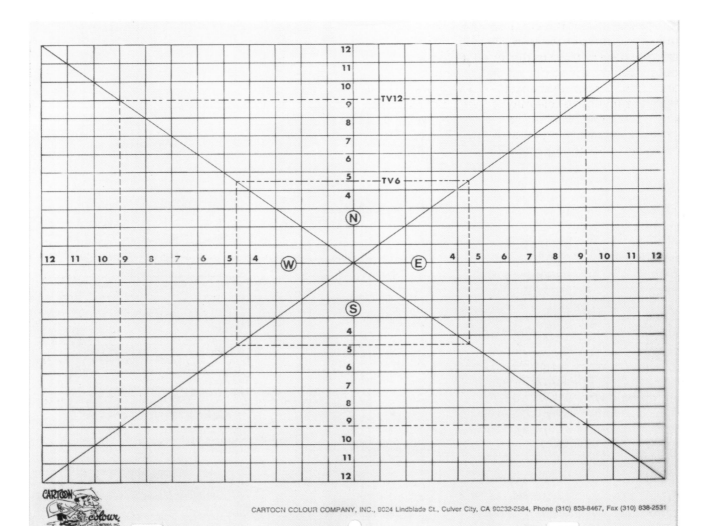

STORYBOARDS AND LAYOUT

The layouts are the technical versions of the storyboards and act as the blueprints for the animators, effects animators, camera operators, and painting department.

The storyboard is a visual shorthand interpretation of the script. Many different approaches are tried in the storyboard stage before one is settled on. It's an important and creative step. In the storyboard below, from the inventive television series *Dexter's Lab,* you can see that the storyboard artist varies the camera angles, as well as the size of the shots, creating a zippy, stylish scene.

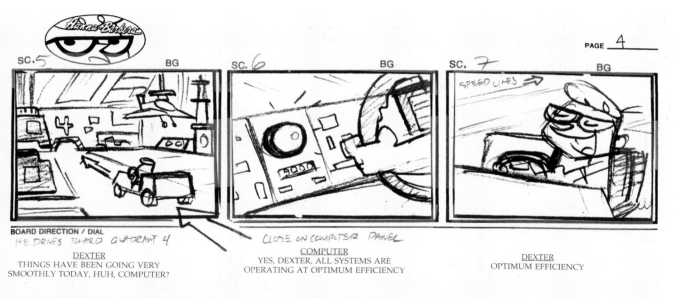

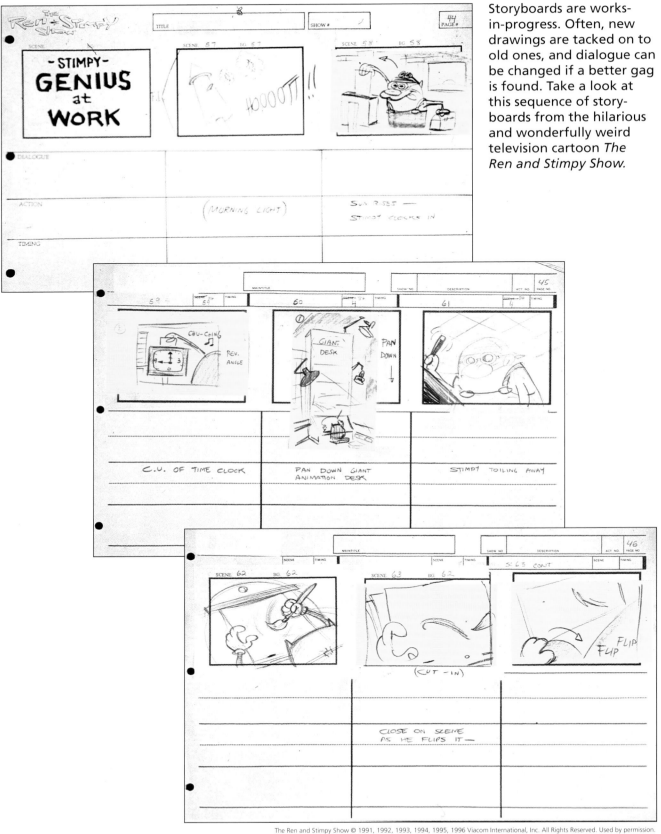

Storyboards are works-in-progress. Often, new drawings are tacked on to old ones, and dialogue can be changed if a better gag is found. Take a look at this sequence of storyboards from the hilarious and wonderfully weird television cartoon *The Ren and Stimpy Show*.

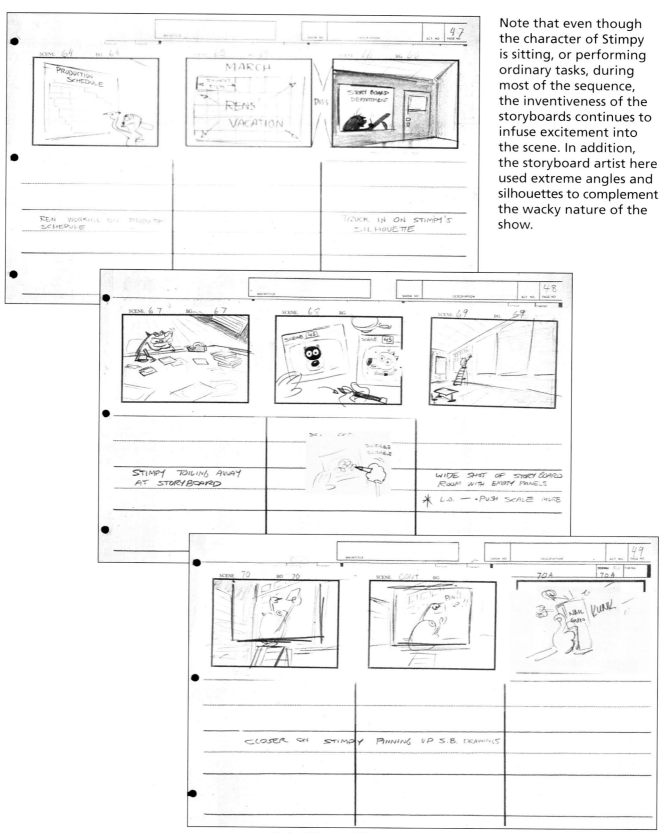

Note that even though the character of Stimpy is sitting, or performing ordinary tasks, during most of the sequence, the inventiveness of the storyboards continues to infuse excitement into the scene. In addition, the storyboard artist here used extreme angles and silhouettes to complement the wacky nature of the show.

THE LAYOUT ARTIST

Layout artists create the settings in which the animated characters will perform; they're the architects of the scenes. They help to create and establish the mood, atmosphere, time, place, scale, pattern of action, lighting, camera angle, and style of a scene.

Prerequisites for being a layout artist are, first of all, drawing ability (the better draftsman you are, the easier it is to communicate your ideas), plus a knowledge of perspective, composition and design, research, film editing and cutting, art techniques or style, and animation and the camera.

COMPOSITION AND DESIGN: UNDERSTANDING THE WORK AREA

A good composition has a variety of sizes and spaces, and makes use of positive as well as negative space. I recommend taking a good design class. It will teach you about shape, space, color, composition, and visual communication.

DESIGN DO'S AND DON'TS

Here are a few guidelines to keep in mind when designing your space.

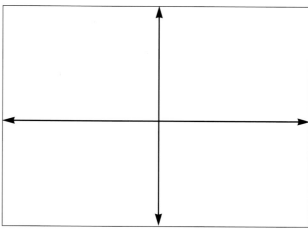

DON'T divide the area equally, either horizontally or vertically.

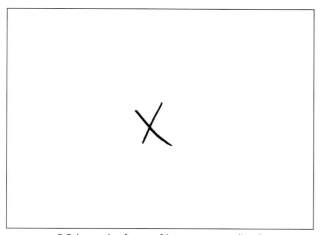

DO keep the focus of interest centralized.

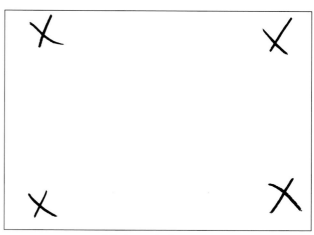

DO stay out of corners.

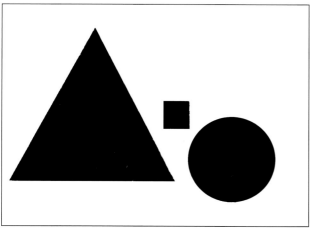

DO use a variety of shapes and sizes.

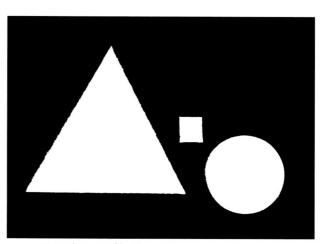

DO make use of both positive and negative space.

BE CREATIVE

Bear in mind, that in layout as well as in animation, you're not drawing actual trees, houses, and characters, but are simply creating shapes (to the best of your ability) that recognizably represent these three-dimensional objects on a two-dimensional surface. With this in mind, you can approach your work in a more open-minded manner, instead of limiting yourself to photo-realistic representations.

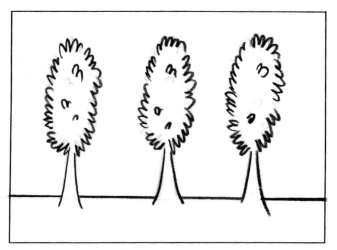

Having three trees all the same size and the same distance apart makes this composition static and boring.

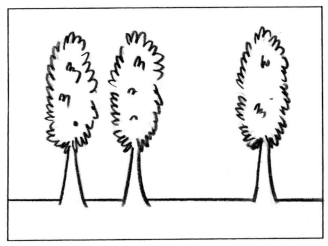

Rearranging them using a variety of negative spaces creates a more interesting composition.

Varying the sizes of the trees results in an even more artistic composition and also gives the illusion of depth.

Applying three different values (light, medium, and dark) not only creates more depth, but suggests lighting and direction, as well.

STAGING AND FRAMING

Deciding what the camera should see for each scene is the layout artist's responsibility. He or she determines the camera angle, and how and where the camera moves. These moves are broken down into types of shots, very similar to live action camera work:

THE LONG SHOT
TRUCK
TILT
CLOSE UP
DOWN SHOT
SWISH
PAN
UP SHOT
CAMERA JAR

MORE DO'S AND DON'TS

DON'T position the balance of weight of the central character of a shot in the center of the working area. This tends to cramp the character and action.

BETTER VARIETY OF NEG. SPACE

MORE SPACE

CHAR. HAS ROOM TO ACT.

DO place the character's weight off center. Create a feeling of more space in front than in back. Variety in the spaces is more interesting.

PANNING: THE FLOW OF DESIGN

Panning is when the camera turns from one image and focuses on another. When you pan from point A to point B with a live-action camera, the camera lens automatically records every image before it in the viewfinder. In animation, you have to draw every image to create the panning effect.

When you have a pan in your animation, you're giving your character a chance to move around from one position to another. The problem in designing and drawing a pan is to produce movement without jitters (an uncomfortable strobe effect for the viewer). Jitters are produced by placing verticals on horizontals and arranging objects of the same size in distance of equal space.

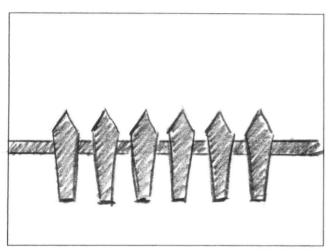

A basic picket fence.

Varying the distance and angles of the slats in the fence creates interest and flow in the pan.

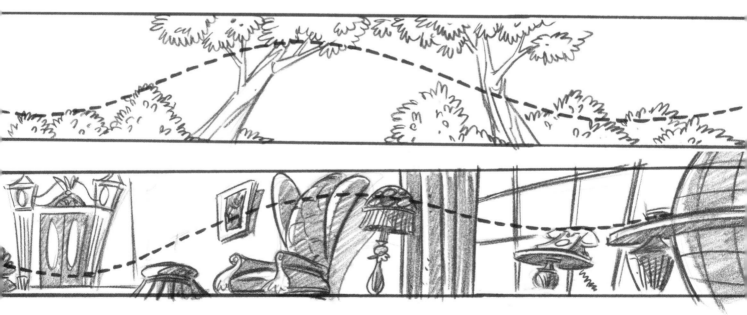

The best movements and layouts in panning are obtained by angling and slanting objects. Think in terms of flowing through an imaginary curved line, and place objects to follow that curve. The speed of the pan will determine the degree of slant. If the speed of the pan is faster, the slant is greater.

CONTRAST AND SCALE

Think of contrast in terms of opposing elements. It adds interest, communicates ideas, and gives the composition a stronger impact (as in the bottom illustration). If every character looked, sounded, and moved alike on the same background, your ideas would be boring and repetitive. By using contrasting elements, you can achieve an unlimited amount of communication and entertainment value.

STYLE, MOOD, AND ATMOSPHERE

There are many different styles and moods in animation, including realism, extreme realism, simplified realism, suggestion, graphic, literal, fantasy, realistic fantasy, formal, cartoony, expressionistic, and caricatured, among many others. The style of the layout is determined by many factors, including story, characters, and color. A specific style and atmosphere is usually arrived at by altering either shapes, surface patterns, subjects, or a combination of these things. Compare the examples of different atmospheres in the drawings below.

RENDERING

Rendering is an important skill. However, careful rendering cannot save a badly conceived design and composition; the rendering of a scene is always secondary in importance to the layout. Below are the different types of rendering styles.

You can achieve this linear, cross-hatch effect using a sharp pencil point.

A bold approach results in a strong and dynamic look.

To get a softer look, use the side of the pencil.

A chiseled line suggests tone.

You must establish a strong foundation of composition, light, shade, shape, and values in rough form before you can begin rendering.

One of the greatest difficulties in rendering is knowing when to stop. Eventually, experience will tell you when you've worked enough. Say the most with the least.

The layout artist's job in rendering is to communicate to the other departments; layouts aren't meant to be framed and hung up in an art gallery—although, the way animation art is selling nowadays . . . you never know!

BACKGROUNDS

A finished background, like a good musical score, can be the element that adds that extra charm, warmth, storybook quality, or cutting-edge feel to a story. Take a look at this terrific background from *Dexter's Lab*. Every gadget looks like it has a purpose; it all belongs together. And, it's *fun.*

Background painters really do a job when they bring the black-and-white drawings to fruition with color. And, the painters don't always come from animation backgrounds; many have experience in fine arts.

H00651-96003   " QUADRANT 4 ENTRANCE "   BG-5

H00651-96003   " QUAD 4 ENTRANCE "   BG-5

BACKGROUND DISTORTION

In order to mimic a live-action camera lens, this sweeping background below (from the movie *Fieval Goes West*) is distorted in the middle. Similarly, if you were to show a tilt up from a tall building, you'd draw the building to swell in the middle in order to mimic the lens distortion of live action.

CHOOSE APPROPRIATE ANGLES

Always choose angles that are appropriate for your characters. This shot of Fieval, from *Fieval Goes West,* is low to the ground, giving us the mouse's point of view. We're definitely in his world here, not the world of humans. If this were a story about a giant, a severe down shot would be in order.

When you watch animated movies in which humans and their pets lead parallel lives, watch for the camera angles; you'll know from the height of the camera when the director wants you to see things from a human's point of view or from a pet's point of view.

STRAIGHT FROM HOLLYWOOD:

AN INTERVIEW WITH ROGER ALLERS

Roger Allers is one of the top animation directors today. He has co-directed the highest grossing animated film of all time, Disney's *The Lion King*. In this interview, he graciously shares his professional insights, as well as gives valuable advice and encouragement for aspiring artists.

Chris Hart: Roger, could you give some advice to the person who's reading this book and wants to get into the business?

Roger Allers: Maybe one thing that's encouraging is that I didn't go to an animation school. I just had a very ordinary kind of education. I went to Arizona State University and majored in drawing and painting. It's funny because, during my childhood, I was always focused toward animation. I thought I was going to become an animator. And then, when I got to high school, [Walt] Disney died. And I said, "Oh", and kind of gave up on the idea. So I just pursued painting and drawing, which I would certainly recommend to anybody. Good courses on life drawing are invaluable, all drawing, and any kind of art history—as much as people can educate themselves in terms of understanding everything about the world of art and history.

CH: What was your first job, professionally?

RA: I was in Boston, and I heard about an animation studio there and just took down my college portfolio. (I had sat in on an animation class at Harvard. I wasn't a Harvard student at the time, but the teacher looked at my drawings and said, "Come sit in on my class.") I had done a little 15-second film in that class. So, I took that and my portfolio down

and got hired by a little studio in Boston.

We were doing children's educational shows, commercials. Probably, people won't even remember these shows: *The Electric Company* and *Make a Wish,* things like that. They required a certain amount of animation. Each animator would get his own show, because there would maybe be a total of a minute or two. So, when I started off, I did everything from storyboarding to the pencil animation to the inking and painting and, finally, shooting. And it was a great start for someone in animation, because I learned about all aspects.

I worked as an animator on *Animal Olympics,* which was a series that sort of got squashed by the canceling of the Olympics at the time, and on another thing, *Rock and Rule* in Canada with Nelvana. I had a string of things that never seemed to make it to the screen. As a matter of fact, there was about a seven-year period in which everything I worked on never seemed to make it to the screen. I also worked on *Little Nemo*.

After so many years and nothing getting on the screen, you start asking yourself, "Am I really doing the right thing?" And, I had to admit to myself that I loved what I did, even though it was frustrating and wasn't getting on the screen. So, from there I came to Disney. I found out they had an opening position for a story man, and I applied. That was during *Oliver & Company*. And, I was hired to do story.

CH: Was that doing storyboards?
RA: Yes. So I did that on *Oliver &*

Company. Did it on *The Little Mermaid.* And I was basically a storyman on every picture up until *The Lion King*.

CH: That's interesting for the readers to learn. Most people think you have to go in as an animator, but there are other areas.
RA: Absolutely. Some people have become directors from being animators. Several people have come from story. I had never directed actors before, although I had certainly worked with all the story people before. In a way, a lot of the storyboard artists are actors. They're creating characters and working up business and dialogue and all that, so in a way that's part of acting.

Lots of times, the live-action voice actors are unavailable. They're busy with commitments in movies and it's hard to get to them for these recording sessions. So, when you're in recording with them, you take that opportunity to try to get as many different ways of covering lines as you can—as many different interpretations—and then you go back and try to make sense out of it, try to find the best performance. It's hard . . . since you're often recording them individually, you've got to match them to another character in the same scene who's recorded at a different time. That's tricky.

CH: How do you work with the layout people?
RA: It sort of starts in story. In story, you work out a sequence. And, some story artists are very film oriented; their minds are very good at describing something. And, if you're looking at the storyboard, it starts to

suggest how the film will actually move, in terms of the scenes and cutting and everything.

CH: So, the storyboard artist is giving you the concept on how to get the point across and the layout person is giving you the execution.
RA: Right. The layout artist is really, in a way, the filmmaker. In a lot of ways, the layout artists at the studio are like the directors of photography on a live-action picture. They have to come up with the ideas of how to break up the levels and move them at different paces to create the sense of moving through a three-dimensional universe. All we're using are generally flat, two-dimensional planes of artwork, even though we do use the computer for some things; mostly, it's all traditional artwork. In that way, the layout artist brings the eye of the camera to it.

CH: It's such a collaborative effort. Newer artists may be a bit surprised when they come from working in their room, alone, making hundreds and hundreds of drawings and shooting it themselves, to going to an animation studio where everything is like a beehive of activity, everybody working together.
RA: It really is, and I think it's easier for some people than others. Some artist may come into this environment and not find it satisfying because it is such a group work—you know, to see that their design ideas are also going to be influenced by other people. In a way, it's tricky for an artist, because of the artist's ego. A lot of times in this collaborative way that we work, we're all adding to the final result. A story person, from that point of view, is just the beginning of the plant. You're the seed or you're the early sprout, and when the thing finally turns into a tree, it may not look, on the surface, anything like what it was when you worked on it, but what you are is the understructure that got it that far along.

So, a lot of times people can't just point to the screen and say, "I did that," because what you're seeing is not exactly what they've done. Certainly, the clean-up artists get to point up there and say, "Those are my drawings up there." I think in some ways that's a large part of the satisfaction for those people, who do a job that a lot of people think is such incredible work. They do have the satisfaction of seeing their beautiful drawings up on the screen.

CH: Can you describe the rank of job titles in animation?
RA: There's the animator. Within that there are lead animators, who can oversee a whole character (kind of lead the whole troop), and there are the other animators who work on that character. Then there are animating assistants. This doesn't mean they're assisting on the animator's scenes; these are animators doing their own scenes, but they're generally people who are not as experienced. The lead animator, sort of looking over them, is there to help them out.

Then, you start getting to your assistants and your in-betweeners, who are working on the scenes that the animators are doing. And, I have to say that working as an assistant or an in-betweener for a really great animator is also really educational.

CH: What are the qualities you look for when hiring an animator?
RA: The first thing I look for, in someone's portfolio, is expressive drawing. Does the drawing express a sense of weight or character or an attitude? Does the person have an expressive line? Gesture drawing? Things like that. Are they able to communicate not just a sense of three-dimensional solidity, but even more importantly, expressions of emotions through posture and pose. The main thing I think is expressiveness. Can someone communicate that? It's all about communication. So, you look to see who can communicate and who has fun ideas. Is there anything in their portfolio that makes you laugh? That's another aspect. Or, is there anything that makes you say, "That's a beautiful line. Look how that describes the backbone of that animal." So, I would look for expressive, communicative design.

And I look to see how people's minds work. Are they just trying to copy other people's work, or are they original, thinking people? Is there a personality that's expressed through their drawings?

CH: Say you're starting out. You're a young artist, and you approach the studios for work. What kind of portfolio should you have? Must you always have a sample reel of actual animation, or if you don't have that, can a portfolio of illustrations be sufficient? And, what kind of illustrations would you include?
RA: It's useful, if you want to become an animator, to have a reel of some animation. It's not necessary. A person could submit a portfolio that has a wealth of gesture drawings and life studies, such as human and animal figures.

CH: How much animation does someone usually produce a week if they're an animator?
RA: Oh boy, does that vary! Sometimes it's as little as a foot. But, I'd say it ranges anywhere from 2 feet to, in the crunch, 10 or 12 feet of film a week. It's 18 frames per foot, so if you roughly consider 18 drawings a foot. . . . And, it's really not so much the number of drawings—because you'll produce more than that just trying to get to those 18—the main thing is getting those 18 to work and communicate.

CH: What kind of training should an animator have?
RA: In terms of animation programs, I know that Cal Arts [in Valencia] has a good program out here in California. Sheridan [in Ontario] has a good program up in Canada. Those are the two main ones that I know about. I'm sure there are others. And, as I said, you don't necessarily have to go to a school that teaches animation if your drawing skills are developed enough. But, definitely, I'd recommend all kinds of drawing, especially lots of life drawing, and also, things that come in handy for animators and story people alike are studying drama, because really, an animator is an actor, in a way. And, a really great sense of music is really handy.

INDEX

CREDITS

Christopher Hart: pages 1-4, 6, 8-15, 18-39, 45-51, 60-62, 64-82, 84-105, 112, 113

Nancy Beiman: pages 16, 17, 114-123

Chrystal Klabunde: pages 40-44, 52-55, 58, 59, 63

Guy Vasilovich: pages 131-139

Doug Compton: pages 56 (bottom), 57 (bottom), 106-111, 124, 125

Larry Leichliter: pages 56 (top), 57 (top)